A PRACTICAL GUIDE

52 of the UK's Most Unforgettable Experiences

Achievable Adventures

CHARLIE WILD + JESSICA LAST

QUADRILLE

To Sonny Wild, who joined us halfway through this book,
and in doing so delayed its release by many months.

We won't hold it against you.

Mum & Dad x

Introduction

This is a collection of 52 of our favourite UK Achievable Adventures. By sharing them we hope to show that regular adventure doesn't have to be exclusive to intrepid explorers, big budgets or faraway lands and that there are, in fact, plenty of incredible options right here on our doorstep for everyone to enjoy. Furthermore, through this book, we want to prove that by taking fewer aeroplanes you can forge more sustainable travel habits, without sacrificing experience.

We have spent the last three years exploring the UK in search of unique and exciting possibilities; from climbing the peaks of the Scottish Highlands to surfing the breaks off Northern Ireland, foraging the deepest forests of Snowdonia to camping wild on Dartmoor, we have uncovered a spread of incredible adventures that have completely changed the way we view the UK.

We hope this book inspires you to seek out your own experiences and take full advantage of this set of islands we are lucky enough to call home.

Who are we?

We are Charlie and Jess, founders of The Travel Project and champions of what we call Achievable Adventure.

A few years ago we realized that what makes us happiest is having regular adventure in our lives - quite simple, really. Except, of course, it's not, as this lifestyle is completely unrealistic long-term. The cost and time challenges forced us to reimagine what adventures looked like, scaling them back and exploring closer to home, meaning that we were able to fit regular doses into our weekends and spare time. This, in turn, had a hugely positive impact on both our physical and mental health, while at the same time creating a more sustainable way for us to explore.

In a nutshell, we believe that adventure is good for you, and, if you keep it local, it's good for the planet, too.

The more we experienced, the more we were hooked and so decided to set ourselves a challenge to see just how much the UK has to offer - could we complete 52 UK adventures in 52 weeks? This slightly mad plan exceeded all expectations, opening our eyes to the incredible landscapes, communities, wildlife and experiences the UK has to offer. And, to be honest, it also revealed just how little we knew about the country we were both born in and it hammered home how accessible all these incredible places are for us.

The year was nothing short of life-changing. It made us realize that we had only just scratched the surface and so we decided to continue the project, searching up and down the UK, uncovering the best adventures in our weekends and spare time.

And now it's time to share our findings with you.

What are Achievable Adventures?

Think of Achievable Adventures as a new approach to adventure. Instead of heading out on only one a year, it can be a monthly, if not weekly part of your schedule - a regular opportunity to push yourself out of your comfort zone, even if only slightly, and enjoy the benefits of doing so. Achievable Adventures are personal and scalable; some of them are doable in a few hours, while for others we'd recommend you take a few days. That flexibility is key - the adventures need to fit realistically into your everyday life.

And these experiences are for everyone. We want to bin the idea that you need to be an 'adventure person' and empower everyone to get out and enjoy the outdoors in a way that works for them. Achievable Adventures are designed to offer a spread of genuinely exciting outdoor experiences for people of all tastes and appetites, allowing you to get your fix in a way that suits you.

This stripped-back approach doesn't require long aeroplane journeys to the other side of the world and doesn't need to cost you an arm and a leg.

Finally, this book is designed to get you away from screens and into the outdoors. By getting outside regularly and exposing yourself to new experiences, environments and people, you build mental and physical resilience, reduce stress, gain perspective and create moments that will last far longer than any suntan. We believe that everyone should be able to enjoy these benefits.

And so, by showcasing a range of genuinely achievable UK adventures, we hope to open up the outdoors to everyone and show you the incredible possibilities we have here on our shores.

Adventure in the UK

If we had to sum up the UK's adventure scene in one word, it would be 'underrated'.

For such a small place, there's a bewildering amount to discover. The archipelago of Britain has over 6000 islands and the UK comprises four countries, each with their own distinct cultures and diverse landscapes. We have several seas, an ocean, and the English Channel. There are some 120 mountains over 600 metres high that you can summit and 15 incredible national parks to explore.

Put it this way, you could explore for a lifetime and still not get bored.

How to use this book

While trying to make this book as useful as possible, we asked ourselves one key question: 'What book do we wish we'd had while on our adventures?' In doing so, hopefully we've struck a balance between information and inspiration, giving you bite-sized breakdowns which will enable you to head out and enjoy the UK for yourselves.

We've decided to divide the book by country, to make it easier to link experiences together on a long weekend or week off work. As a reminder, it's by no means an exhaustive list of what you can do in the UK and we're sure you'll find your own adventures along the way – in fact, that's very much part of the fun.

Each adventure includes a breakdown of key details to help you understand how suitable it is for you. It covers the key questions you're likely to have when deciding on an adventure. How long will it take? Is it very physically demanding? How much is it likely to cost? How much effort will it take to plan, or to get to? Do I need to bring any kit? And what's the transport situation?

Here's how we break it down:

___

Time Few hours / Full day / Multi-day.

___

Fitness Low / Medium / High.
We are in no way athletes, but we're young(ish) and able-bodied, and have made these categorizations based on our personal experience.

___

Cost Free / Affordable / Costly.
Note that 'free' does not account for transport costs or general sustenance throughout the day, only the activity in question.

___

Effort Low / Medium / High.
This denotes how much pre-planning and overall time and energy you will need to put into the adventure.

___

Equipment Required / Some recommended / None.
We define 'equipment' as anything outside of the usual useful things that we always carry in our bags (page 222).

___

Transport Public transport available / Best by car / Car required.

___

You'll also find Adventure Resources at the end of the book. This is your quick and easy reference for all the adventures.

England

Size 50,301 square miles
(130,278 sq km)

National parks 10
(covering 10% of
land area)

**UNESCO World Heritage
Sites** 19

Highest peak Scafell Pike
(978m)

Dark Sky Reserves 6

Largest lake Windermere
(10.5 miles long and
1 mile wide /17 km long
and 1.5 km wide)

A dawn dip at Pedn Vounder

Let's not beat about the bush – this is one of the UK's most spectacular beaches. It has it all: shallow, crystal-clear waters; a pristine stretch of golden sand; and an extraordinary location at the foot of dramatic Cornish cliffs. For us the feeling of visiting Pedn Vounder is a little different to any other beach, starting from the audible 'wow' moment as you catch your first glimpse from the clifftop. Swimming in these waters is a real British bucket list tick.

Time few hours

Fitness medium

Cost free

Effort medium

Equipment none

Transport best by car

Is this for me?

Firstly, it's worth noting that this isn't exactly England's easiest beach to get to. Located right out on the far southwestern tip of the UK, Pedn Vounder is nowhere near any major cities – or even towns for that matter. What's more, actually getting down to the beach from the clifftop coast path requires scrambling down a rocky trail, and even climbing in places. If you aren't confident, have restricted mobility, or are travelling with small children, then this might be quite a tricky spot for you to reach.

That said, if you're up for it, then the journey to Pedn Vounder is very much part of the adventure – and the payoff is spectacular, and more than worth the effort.

The adventure

To get to Pedn Vounder, head first to the small village of Treen; you can leave your car in a car park here. The clifftop is about ten minutes' walk through the village, along well-trodden tracks lined with sea thrift. Once you reach the coast the drama really begins, as you round the corner and catch your first glimpse of the beach almost 20 metres below. The view is breathtaking, if a little knee-wobbling!

At this point you will realize that you are most certainly not there yet, and reaching the beach itself will require you to navigate some trickier terrain. The route down is fairly obvious, and will lead you over rocks and through narrow gaps before landing you about five metres above the beach at another sensational viewpoint. The last leg is even more precarious, requiring you to climb down a steep section using your hands and feet to feel your way. It isn't the toughest climb, but it definitely demands you concentrate in order to avoid doing yourself an injury.

Now you've made it down, a real sense of achievement sets in – you've come a long way for this moment! And it won't disappoint as you feel the sand between your toes and strip off for a swim in that deliciously clear water.

Now, it's at this point that we should probably mention a couple of key things. Firstly, due to the beauty of Pedn Vounder, it has become increasingly well-known in recent years. It's still no Fistral Beach, but it can get really busy depending on the time of year or even the day you visit. So, as with many of our adventures, we got ourselves out of bed at the crack of dawn to make sure we had the whole place to ourselves. It was more than worth it. Secondly, Pedn Vounder is set on a sandbar which is not fully revealed until low tide, so to see the beach at its most stunning, try to get there when the water is out. That said, on our arrival at high tide on a misty morning, we still found it to be incredible.

Don't forget

From a safety perspective, the most important thing is proper footwear. With that rocky scramble down to the sand, flip flops are just not going to cut it! You should also pack your swimmers – trust us, you don't want to make it all the way down to this gem and realize that you can't get in the water... That said, if you do forget them, no one will mind if you take a dip anyway – Pedn Vounder is also a nudist beach, so if you want to feel really free then perhaps you won't be needing any clothes at all. Please do be considerate of this fact, especially when it comes to taking photos, and respect people's privacy.

Tracing centuries-old tracks through the forests of the Lake District, your pace dedicated by your pony, is the very definition of a slow adventure. A journey back in time as much as through the English mountains, this meditative adventure opens your eyes to a simpler, older and altogether wilder version of the UK.

Time full day / multi-day

Fitness medium

Cost affordable

Effort medium

Equipment none

Transport car required

Cumbria, England

Fell pony trekking across the Lake District

Is this for me?

This trip is easy to adapt to your schedule, fitness level and appetite for adventure, with everything from day treks through to three-night wild camping trips available. Public transport around here is pretty fragmented, so it's tough to do without a car.

Even if you aren't a 'horse person' per se, you'll find that the ponies provide a lot of value. They carry all the kit and supplies, freeing you up to enjoy the journey; they set a slow and steady pace which forces you into a therapeutic rhythm; and finally, you will undoubtedly find yourself forming a bond with these kind characters. This adventure is for those who want something a little different, a memorable way to absorb the history and beauty of northwest England.

The adventure

To understand the unique nature of this adventure, you must first know a little bit about Tom, the founder of Fell Pony Adventures. He leads all the treks, and his vision is integral to the experience. Not only is he one of the nicest and most interesting people you're likely to meet, but he has an incomparable passion and knowledge for fell ponies, passed down in his family for generations.

Indigenous to Cumbria and the lakes, the ponies are strong, hardy and intelligent, with muscular, stocky builds and silky manes. Unfortunately however, they are becoming increasingly rare, something Tom is on a mission to change. He hopes to raise the profile of the ponies by using them to help reconnect people with nature in this dramatic corner of Britain.

All the treks start from Tom's yard, just a 10-minute drive from the very southern tip of Lake Windermere. Preparation depends on the length of your adventure, but all will require comfortable hiking boots, plus a waterproof just in case! After being introduced to the ponies you'll learn how to load them up with your kit – you won't be riding them, but walking alongside them as they carry your gear. With this done, it's time to stride out into the wilds of the Lake District, leaving civilization behind.

You will quickly become familiar with Tom's character and the immense value he brings to the experience, as he educates you in his soft tones on the history of the area and the ponies. It will take you next to no time to slip into the rhythm dictated by your new equine companion, a leisurely pace which might just be the key to Tom's calming energy. It's a luxuriously slow-paced way to enjoy one of England's most breathtaking locations.

Whichever trek you're on, the adventure will take you up and along the old pathways, weaving through forests and across fells. We were struck by the majestic scale of this environment and the sense of possibility as we encountered rolling vista after rolling vista. This really is wild England at its natural best.

When it's time to eat, Tom takes you to a picturesque spot where you take the packs off the ponies and let them graze for a while. Lunch comprises homemade soup, local cheeses and breads (can be personalized for those with specific dietary requirements). This break in the action offers a moment to take stock of the experience so far.

We only had time for a one-day trek, so spent the afternoon gently working our way back down to the yard. But if we'd had more time we would without a doubt have tried a two- or three-day experience, setting up camp in extraordinary spots each evening, cooking on an open fire and trading stories from the day's adventure.

People who have gone on these longer treks say that returning to 'normal life' is almost a bit tricky, and they yearn to be back out on the fells. Although we wished it had been longer, our single-day adventure was still incredible, leaving us recharged and looking with fresh eyes at the country we were born in.

Don't forget

Whatever the weather, make sure you wear sturdy boots. You will be covering all types of terrain and so will need boots that ensure comfort and support throughout.

Slow living at Settle

Rarely does a place get it this right. It's the attention to detail on all fronts, from design to guest experience, that makes this woodland gem one of the very best experiential stays in England. A weekend spent here will relax you in ways not many others could, drawing you closer to nature and allowing you to completely switch off from the outside world – a gloriously slow adventure.

Time	multi-day
Fitness	low
Cost	costly
Effort	low
Equipment	none
Transport	public transport available

Is this for me?

Due to its popularity, the main barrier to entry with this adventure is availability. In the summer months and on weekends it can be tricky to get a spot at Settle – though they do offer a bell tent option in summer now, which has increased their capacity. However, with trains from King's Cross to nearby Attleborough and an extremely slow pace of life once you've arrived, this adventure is easy to achieve for most people. So, if you are looking for a couple's getaway or an adventurous experience with minimal planning, this is for you.

The adventure

Settle is a beautifully curated collection of stays tucked away in private parkland near Attleborough in the depths of central Norfolk. The best way to get there is by car, as it gives you the freedom to move around once you arrive. However the nearest train station is Attleborough, which is only a 15-minute taxi journey from Settle. Plus, if you're anything like us then you won't be needing your vehicle much once you arrive, as you will most likely just want to relax and make the most of this beautiful space.

Settle comprises three vintage railway carriages, several luxury bell tents and a lakeside cabin – all converted into unique places to spend the night. With a range of options, Settle caters for a spread of needs and budgets, starting from around £100 for the bell tents and running through to the more luxury end of the market with the lakeside cabin.

Refurbished railway carriages seem to be everywhere at the moment. These, however, are on a whole other level. Every detail is designed to make your stay ridiculously comfortable. From the weathered wood to whittled stools and timeless textures – every feature is faultlessly considered. It all combines to create a space that, once you factor in the wood-burning stove, you won't want to leave.

If you visit in the summer months, you might want to consider staying in one of the bell tents. These spacious canvas safari tents get you even closer to nature, and are perfect for admiring the night sky. In keeping with Settle's signature obsession with comfort, they have excellent mattresses, their own electricity supply, and a personal yoga deck complete with fire pit and deck chairs.

In our case, we stayed at the lakeside cabin, spending among the most relaxing two nights we've ever had. After stepping through the cabin's large sliding glass doors, you're met with a large open-plan kitchen and living room space, with views over its doorstep lake. Off the bedroom is an en-suite bathroom with a luxurious standalone bath. Our favourite parts were outside of the cabin, though: the deck complete with a formidable BBQ and dining area and the private lakeside wood-fired bath. There's no better place to sip wine and watch the birds swoop down to your lily pad-covered lake for an evening drink of their own.

No matter which of the three options you go for, you are free to explore the surrounding grounds as you wish. Check out the surrounding woodland and lakes for a stroll. Visit the on-site honesty shop to pick up locally sourced supplies. Or even have your own farm-to-table experience via the small herb and salad garden where you can pick beautifully fresh ingredients. What's more, upon arrival you will receive a hamper containing fresh butter, eggs, bread and porridge oats – everything you need to start the day.

Throughout this book, we've recommended a lot of high-tempo, adrenaline-fuelled adventures. This one is the polar opposite. It is as slow as an adventure can go, giving you the chance to take a break from reality and slip into another world, one which moves at a more sedate pace. What an excellent use of the Norfolk countryside.

Don't forget

Make sure you book in advance to avoid disappointment. They do sometimes have last-minute cancellations, though, so follow Settle Norfolk on Instagram for the chance to snap one up! Once booked, it's worth grabbing some food and drinks from a supermarket en route. Yes, they have some supplies on-site, but for this trip you'll want to indulge.

There's something quintessentially British about the idea of laying out a picnic blanket on top of Kent's iconic white cliffs, scoffing sandwiches as you gaze out over the English Channel. Add in the drama of a sunset, and you have an adventure which is both memorable and easily achievable. What's not to like?

Time	few hours
Fitness	low
Cost	free
Effort	low
Equipment	none
Transport	public transport available

Kent, England

Watching the sunset from the Seven Sisters cliffs

Is this for me?

This adventure is as easy as they come, giving you a great payoff for minimal effort. If you like food, sunsets or great views – and who doesn't? – then we highly recommend it. If you're based in the southeast, that goes double. With good transport links and easy terrain, this is an experience for everyone.

The adventure

Seven Sisters Country Park is on the south coast of England, just a couple of hours by car from London near Seaford, East Sussex. Alternatively, the regular number 12 Coaster Bus from Eastbourne Station takes about half an hour. We tackled this adventure after work, driving down from London to make the most of a long, light summer's evening.

Before you set off we recommend heading to the shops and picking up some food and drinks. Put anything chilled into a cooler with some ice, grab a rug and you're good to go – that's all you will need for the adventure.

If you're driving, park in the carpark near the tiny clifftop village of Birling Gap. Then, start walking east along the clifftop towards the unmistakable Belle Tout Lighthouse, perched right on the cliff edge. If you look down you'll spot the famous red and white stripes of Beachy Head Lighthouse in the ocean below.

The stretch of coastal path that connects Birling Gap and Belle Tout is ideal for watching the sunset; just pick your favourite spot, lay out your rug and enjoy the last of the day's light. As sunset approaches, the waters of the English Channel will seem to swirl with pinks, gold and reds. It is a spectacular sight, and coming to see it makes for a great, inexpensive adventure.

If you want to spend longer here, we'd recommend coming earlier in the day to walk some of the many scenic paths along the coastline. The 100-mile South Downs National Trail passes through here, and following it for a short while is always a great option. You could also visit the nearby Cuckmere Meanders for a walk, or even a swim. These are exactly what their name suggests – large, meandering parts of the Cuckmere River. They're quite an incredible sight from up high, and offer large areas of fairly slow-moving water, perfect for a dip if the weather's nice.

Don't forget

In places, the cliffs reach 160 metres high, so be really careful when it comes to picking your picnic spot. Make sure you are at least a couple of metres back from the edge, and on solid ground. As usual when eating al fresco, be sure to pick up all your rubbish when you leave – even food waste.

Located up in the heights of the Lake District, The Hutte from Hinterlandes is as isolated as it gets. Immersed in the drama of this northwestern corner of England, this is where to go if you're looking to escape distraction. Once you're here, you'll be able to unwind and appreciate life's smaller details.

Time	multi-day
Fitness	medium
Cost	affordable
Effort	medium
Equipment	none
Transport	car required

Cumbria, England

A night off-grid in a Lake District cabin

Is this for me?

Let's face it, bothies aren't for everyone. If you don't fancy the bare-bones experience, but do want the immersion in nature which bothies typically offer, then this cabin is the perfect alternative. In order to ensure sustainable use of the land, the Hutte actually moves location every few months, so each experience is slightly different. When we visited we needed to tackle a 45-minute hike uphill – meaning it wasn't suitable for those with limited mobility.

Wherever the Hutte is located when you visit, there'll be nothing but the cabin, a few sheep and miles of glorious Lake District vistas. The cabin comes equipped with a big comfortable bed and all the amenities you need, and after indulging in its glorious isolation you can return to the popular Keswick area, which is a short drive away.

The adventure

This adventure starts when you set off in the morning in search of this hidden location. The nearest town is Keswick, a bustling little hub in the north of the Lakes. The owners of the cabin will direct you to a location where they will meet you, brief you, and send you on your way. You will be able to park here before taking yourself, bags and all, to your home for the night by following their instructions.

As you'll be sensing by now, this isn't your conventional holiday home rental. This is an end-to-end experience designed to push you outside your comfort zone.

Our trek sent us winding up through the wilds of the Lake District. Each minute, the wilderness became more picturesque. After the near-hour walk, we were greeted with a sensational view over Lake Buttermere. This was our eureka moment: faced with the breathtaking sight, it was clear why we'd gone through the effort to stay here.

After turning one final corner, we were face to face with a quaint but quality wooden cabin. It sat nestled into a dip in the hillside, alongside a couple of trees to provide shelter from the winds.

The Tardis-like inside of the cabin feels much larger than it looks from the outside! That's thanks to the high ceilings and space-saving design. A spacious bed sits at one end, framed by a huge window with views over the hills. It almost acts like a floodlight, bringing a lot of natural light into the room. The other end of the cabin plays host to a bathroom, while in between is the living area with a small wood-burning stove, a sink and a kettle. Don't limit yourself to cooking inside, though! There's a pizza oven stationed outside for alfresco dining.

As comfortable as the cabin may be, the real reason you are up there is to take in the surrounding landscapes, which you'll probably only be sharing with sheep. You can wander for hours on end without anyone encroaching on your new rural home. When you're satisfied, slink back inside and warm up by the fire.

There are a thousand ways to escape the hustle and bustle in the Lake District, but this adventure has one unique quality we can't ignore: you'll avoid all other ramblers, while remaining close to Keswick, making it relatively easy to reach. With that in mind, you can take it slow and soak in the smaller joys of nature without having to travel far from all the conveniences of the area.

This is a cabin that goes far beyond being a place to rest your head. It is an immersive experience, where you absorb some of England's most wholesome vistas.

> **Tip: As mentioned, The Hutte is moved throughout the year to ensure the land is looked after, so your experience might differ slightly from ours. Hinterlandes, the creators of The Hutte, also have a collection of other beautifully thought-out, off-grid accommodation options in the area that are very much worth checking out as well.**

Don't forget

Be sure to bring food supplies, including for pizza, to the cabin. It's wise to bring head torches for night-time exploration. And plenty of layers – you won't want to be caught cold.

The salt marshes off the northern coast of Norfolk are one of England's last true slivers of wilderness. The untamed network of narrow waterways and hidden sandbanks was once the domain of smugglers, and the only way to navigate them is with local expertise. This adventure will see you sailing the waters in a lovingly restored classic working boat complete with deep red sails, and guided by a skipper who knows this part of England like the back of their hand.

Time	few hours / full day
Fitness	low
Cost	costly
Effort	low
Equipment	none
Transport	best by car

Norfolk, England

Sailing Norfolk's salt marshes

Is this for me?

This is a real adventure, the sort where the more you get stuck in, the more you will enjoy it. Set off with the intention of getting your hands dirty. And if plain sailing doesn't sound action-packed enough for you, just tailor your trip to suit your tastes. You could go for a feasting expedition complete with a professional chef and the opportunity to forage for some of your lunch; wild swimming; exploring the salt marshes; or even playing a game of cricket on the sandbars!

It is worth mentioning that this is at the more expensive end of activities in this book. We found it worth every penny, though. What you get for your money won't leave you feeling short-changed. Depending on where you are coming from, public transport is possible to the launch point in Wells-next-the-Sea, but a car is much quicker if you're not coming from nearby.

The adventure

The salt marshes require an expert to navigate, which is why we booked with the Coastal Exploration Company (CEC). Their expeditions start at the small market town of Wells-next-the-Sea, on the north Norfolk coast. Park at one of the waterfront carparks, then grab your supplies and make your way to your boat.

There are a lot of different vessels in the CEC fleet, so you can find one to suit your group size and plans. The four-person mussel and crab boats are at the smaller end, while the Victorious, a 100-year-old, thirteen-metre Norfolk smack (traditional shrimping boat), can fit up to eight people. The smaller boats are best for navigating the narrow backwaters, and the larger ones are better suited to sailing the open ocean. As we were keen to explore the salt marshes, we picked a mussel flat boat.

Preparation is very easy. The main requirement is to dress for the weather – the rest will be taken care of by the CEC. If you're going on this adventure in the summer, make sure to bring a swimming costume – but pack warm layers as well!

Next it's time to meet your skipper, learn the basics of the boat and leave the harbour. The mussel boat uses a motor to travel a safe distance out to sea; then, you raise the sails. That's how you know the adventure has really begun. The sails are a work of art in themselves – massive and made of blood-red canvas.

With the wind in your sails, it isn't long before you reach the narrow channels of the salt marshes. These waters are treacherous due to the hidden sandbars that lie beneath the surface. The CEC inspect every spit and bar themselves, so rest assured there's no risk of running aground! They'll steer you through the channels, even popping out and guiding the boat by hand from time to time.

As you get deeper into the marshes, you leave the modern world behind. Before long, you are completely surrounded by the wilds of north Norfolk's exposed salt marshes, a labyrinth of channels creating a vein-like pattern through the landscape. The complete silence is only interrupted by the sails flapping in the wind and the birds calling overhead – the marshes are a protected wetland area, great for birdwatching. The route takes you along the old smugglers' passages, which your skipper will tell you all about as you go.

No matter which trip you take, the team comes well prepared with an abundance of local produce. They'll bring delicious home-baked cakes and flapjacks, and of course plenty of tea and coffee to keep you hydrated and well-fuelled throughout.

This experience is one that will stay with you for a while after it has finished. The silence. The handsome old boats. The wind in your hair. We completely lost track of time, fully immersed in the landscapes and their unique history. Take this unhurried trip to the beautiful and unique Norfolk coast. You won't regret it.

Don't forget

Pack your camera – if you have a passion for photography then you won't want to miss the chance to capture this adventure.

Cove-hopping on the south Devon coast

With huge rewards for those willing to head slightly off the beaten track, this stretch of Devon coast between Dartmouth and Beesands is lined with hidden coves where you can leap from the rocks into beautiful blue waters... and all for free! It's the perfect way to spend a summer's afternoon.

Time few hours

Fitness medium

Cost free

Effort medium

Equipment none

Transport public transport available

Is it for me?

If you are looking for an easy adventure to tackle with friends or family, then this is an excellent choice. An afternoon of drinking beers (optional) and splashing around in crystal-clear water – what more could you want?

This isn't the most accessible adventure, however, with a fair bit of walking and scrambling involved; if you have restricted mobility then this might not be one for you.

The adventure

Sitting right where the River Dart meets the sea, Dartmouth is a typical seaside town that bursts into life in the summer months. Just south of Dartmoor National Park, it's easily accessible by road, and regular trains run to nearby Totnes from London and Birmingham. There are also several foot and car ferries that run regularly to the harbour from a variety of nearby locations including Totnes and Greenway.

Dartmouth has a classic British summertime atmosphere: sunlit streets lined with colourful buildings; happy punters relaxing on bustling pub terraces; and that mouthwatering scent drifting out of fish and chip shops. But you might be tempted out of town before long, drawn to explore the little stretch of cove-strewn coast nearby.

A picturesque 40-minute walk from town, along the river to the coast, is Dartmouth Castle. The gentle trail hugs the river as it goes, giving you a great view over the water. The River Dart buzzes with life in the summer, with boats, paddle boarders and swimmers all finding a place, adding a lively energy to the route.

The castle itself is an old artillery fort, built in the 1380s to protect against the threat of the French. The small, well-preserved building was carved into the rock of the shoreline, and still sits proudly looking out to sea all these centuries later.

If you want to pick up an afternoon snack, stop at the neighbouring Castle Tea Rooms. Along with well-made coffee, tea and cakes, they serve sandwiches. The handpicked crab sandwich is on another level, a gift from the seafood sarnie gods.

Armed with a full cooler, you just need somewhere picturesque to sit and enjoy your picnic. This is probably a good time to mention that you will certainly not be short of exceptional viewpoints along this route. All of them will be quite tempting to stop at for lunch, but if you are after an escape from the crowds, it's wise to push on a bit further.

From the castle follow the path up and along, and you'll soon find yourselves on the South West Coast Path. By this point the hordes of people will have evaporated, and you will find yourself with only nature for company.

The 630-mile (1,014-km) coast path wraps around the far southwest of mainland Britain, taking in the whole of Cornwall and Devon's spectacular coastlines, plus some scenic sections in Dorset and Somerset. Picking it up here, you'll first pass through some gorgeous forests, but before long it will open up and give you sweeping sea views. The pathway is elevated above the ocean, following the cliff round, with a whole host of coves and rocky outlets down to its left. In the first little stretch alone you have Sugary, Deadmans and Ladies coves, as well as several spots where you can lie out on the rocks and jump into the sea. Once you've had enough of one cove, simply move on around the corner and find a new one!

This adventure is the perfect example of what you can achieve if you push on just a little further than the crowds. The truth is that most people are happy to stick to the beaten path, and feel like veering away from the masses is not worth the effort. Our opinion is the opposite. It's always worth going just that little bit further, and in this case the payoff is brilliant.

Don't forget

Be prepared! It makes the day much more fun if you have some drinks and food with you, allowing you to really settle in and make the most of your time there. Also, don't forget to check the tide times here as some of the coves are best experienced at low tide. Finally, always be careful when sea swimming, as currents can be strong; make sure you are sensible throughout the experience.

Driving the Northumberland 250

This journey takes you on a 250-mile (402-km) loop around Northumberland, England's most northern and most sparsely populated county. Home to the darkest skies in Europe, vast beaches and ancient forests, Northumberland is packed with options for adventure, and this road trip will show you the very best it has to offer.

Time	multi-day
Fitness	low
Cost	cheap
Effort	medium
Equipment	none
Transport	car required

Is this for me?

As this is a road trip, it is by nature pretty straightforward. You can whiz through it, squeezing in as much sweeping Northumberland scenery as you can into a weekend; or you take your time, ramping up the adventure by stopping for hikes, swims and mini expeditions along the way. The loop caters for all types of adventure seekers, from families to those wanting to really push themselves. That said it is of course best tackled in a car, but if you don't have one a bike could be a great option for those who enjoy a challenge.

The adventure

Northumberland is the perfect location to escape the fast pace of everyday life. With beautiful beaches, a vast national park and miles of rolling hills and conifer forests, you aren't exactly short of options for adventure. What's more, Northumberland is home to a network of scenic and relatively empty roads, meaning that it is perfectly set up for a road trip.

It's this set of ingredients which led to the birth of the Northumberland 250, a 250-mile (402-km) route through the very best this northeastern county has to offer. As it's a loop you can start at any point you would like. Coming from East London, we made the five and a half hour drive up to the small town of Rothbury, so we could start the route early in the morning. We decided to make it a five-day road trip, but you can of course increase or decrease that.

From Rothbury, it's an easy 45-minute drive northeast to Northumberland's famous Bamburgh. The beach is nothing short of spectacular, its miles of sand lined by dunes on one side and the North Sea on the other. We recommend spending a couple of hours exploring this vast stretch, taking in the views of the famous castle standing proudly above the sands, and navigating the grassy dune network. If you have time, you can even take a boat trip to see seals and seabirds on the tiny, rocky Farne Islands.

As you drive north from Bamburgh along the coastal section of the 250, we recommend using your navigation app to scout out a few more beaches. We particularly liked Ross Sands, a great off-the-beaten-track spot for a swim.

Not far north of Ross Sands, you'll come to the causeway crossing to Lindisfarne. A small tidal island situated a mile or so off the coast, its alternative name of Holy Island is due to the monastery founded here in the seventh century. Today you can visit the ruins of a twelfth-century priory on the same site, its lofty sandstone arches still standing proud. To the east is craggy Lindisfarne Castle, with its surprising Arts and Crafts-style interiors designed by Lutyens in the 1900s.

Accessible only at low tide, there are two ways to reach Holy Island: by car across the causeway; or on foot, walking for two hours along the sand guided by a series of long sticks protruding from the ground. Needless to say, you have to time your visit carefully.

North of Lindisfarne is the so-called Borderlands section of the route. You could easily spend a couple of days exploring it, driving from Berwick-upon-Tweed on the coast to the edge of Kielder Forest in the west of Northumberland. As the name suggests, the road weaves between England and Scotland, taking you through beautifully unpopulated rolling hills and wild, windblown moorland.

The Kielder area is home to vast forests, the largest man-made lake in Europe and the best Dark Sky Park in England. It's essentially an enormous adventure playground – you could spend a couple of weeks here on the outdoor activities alone. If you're on a slightly tighter schedule, we recommend prioritizing mountain biking. With its network of forest tracks, lakeside trails and hills of all shapes and sizes, Kielder Forest has something for cyclists at all ability levels.

The southernmost section of the Northumberland 250 includes the genteel market town of Hexham, the perfect launch pad from which to explore Hadrian's Wall. Arguably Northumberland's most famous landmark, this extraordinary feat of human engineering stretches over 73 miles, (117 km) and is impressively intact almost 2000 years after it was built.

Don't forget

This is northeast England, so even if you're visiting in the summer, nothing is guaranteed weather-wise. We suggest you take lots of layers, and prepare for all eventualities. The 250 has an abundance of beautiful picnic spots, a glorious experience when the sun is cooperating. We recommend bringing a comfy rug, plus maybe a little gas stove, cooler box and thermos, and simply stopping at shops and markets to stock up on grub as you go.

Sea foraging at Old Harry Rocks

Spend an afternoon in a kayak searching for edible delicacies. You'll be weaving between the iconic Old Harry Rocks, trying to spot tasty morsels below the surface of the sea. This adventure is one of the most memorable ways to spend a summer's day on the south coast.

Time few hours

Fitness medium

Cost affordable

Effort medium

Equipment none

Transport public transport available

Is this for me?

Sea kayaking takes a degree of upper body strength, but you are able to take this at your own pace. If you need to go slow, go slow! That said, although it's unlikely, it's always possible that you'll capsize, so you need to be confident in your ability to swim back to shore. If you feel safe enough, and you have the above skills, then this is a brilliant adventure. Combine the fun of kayaking, the epic location and the satisfaction of foraging for your dinner, and you'll have one brilliant afternoon.

The adventure

The best way to tackle this adventure is with Fore Adventures, based in Swanage right down on the coast near Old Harry. They are incredibly nice as well as knowledgeable. And don't worry – this is nothing like the dreaded group tour dynamic. While there may be other people in your group (sizes differ depending on the adventure you choose), they're excellent at making the experience feel relaxed and easy, like you're going out with a really clued-up local mate.

To get there, head to the carpark at Studland on the Dorset Coast, where you will find a little Fore Adventures office. For those without a car, a train to Bournemouth and then a bus to Beach Road on the 50 Breezer Swanage route is your best option. You won't need to bring much as they supply all the technical gear – just show up already wearing your swimming costume.

41

At the office you'll meet your guide, who will give you a safety briefing as well as your wetsuit and helmet before you all head down to the sand. When you're there, you'll be attaching single fishing lines to the back of each kayak then heading out into the ocean. Due to the shape of the cliffs here, this little bay is pretty well protected, and on a calm day your paddles will glide through the glass-clear water with ease. Whatever the conditions, your guide will keep you in the loop about safety considerations, while sharing their knowledge about local history and the edible goods you can find along the coast.

The UNESCO-designated Old Harry chalk stacks, only a few hundred metres away, are your first stop. You've probably seen pictures of them, or even spotted them from the cliffs, but believe us when we tell you there is nothing like looking up at them from sea level.

Once you're in the shallows at the base of the rocks, it's time to check your fishing lines to see if you have caught anything. In the summer months you could be catching bream, bass, mackerel, rays and dogfish. Some of them, like the bass, are catch and release only; your guide will clarify which is which.

One of the reasons we rate Fore Adventures is that they manage their own fishing and foraging sessions, with a commitment to sustainability and responsible harvesting. This means you don't have to worry about accidentally fishing in protected waters, or taking something you're not supposed to. In these areas they only ID plants for info, and ensure everything is left how it was.

After you've checked your lines, you'll drag your kayak over the shallows between the rocks and pass through the gap to the other side, where you are met with more incredible chalk formations. Here you'll find yourself paddling through a natural arch. There are plenty of pots installed along the reef here, to see what crustaceans they hold. You could even find lobster! Your guide will also teach you about the varieties of seaweeds which grow here. They each have their health benefits, so fill your nets up with plenty for the upcoming feast.

Tip: Fore Adventures also offer plant-based sea-kayaking foraging options, ideal for vegetarians and vegans.

The next couple of hours are spent paddling these gorgeous waters. Forage your fill, and take in all the views before heading back. Once on terra firma it's time to light a Kadai fire bowl and cook up your finds with Fore's resident chef – after all, though foraging is fun, you'll surely want to enjoy the spoils of your hard work! Kick back and enjoy your own catch with a cold drink while looking out over the Jurassic coastline. This adventure has a bit of everything, and will leave you extremely satisfied.

Don't forget

You'll need sun cream and lots of water, and if you own a pair of waterproof shoes then take them! They'll save your feet when you get out of the kayaks at some points to scramble across rocks.

Hidden in an abandoned slate quarry on Cornwall's wild north coast lies an off-grid escape designed to embed you deep within nature. Comprising four geometric tree-top pods, several tipis and an extraordinary woodland cabin, Kudhva was built in harmony with the existing landscape. The way the site blends seamlessly into its surroundings gives guests a real feeling of natural connection, and easy access to outdoor activities.

Time multi-day	
Fitness medium	
Cost affordable	
Effort low	
Equipment none	
Transport public transport available	

Cornwall, England

A night at Kudhva

Is this for me?

If you want to immerse yourself in nature without sacrificing style, then Kudhva is the place for you. It lives up to its name, which is Cornish for 'hideout'. Set in a 45-acre abandoned quarry overlooking the sea, this off-grid campsite makes sustainability a priority, with shared toilets (some compostable), its own natural water supply and solar power. There are several accommodation options, all perfect for couples and families alike – though if using a ladder or stairs is an issue for you, we suggest opting for a tipi rather than a Kudhva or the Danish Cabin.

What really sets Kudhva apart is its atmosphere. There's just something special about this place, and it's all down to the founder, Louise. Her warmth, creativity and love of life and nature permeates everything and everyone around her, and it's this feeling which has kept us going back year after year.

The adventure

Once you're almost here, your navigation app will lead you to a small signposted turning off the road, where you will drive a short distance up a bumpy slate track to the carpark. The adventure starts with a steep uphill walk through the trees to the heart of the Kudhva camp. Here you will find a fire pit, an outdoor eating area and a large wooden building housing a communal kitchen and hangout space, all within the forest. As well as any other campers, you might spot a couple of goats on your way – they munch their way around the site, preventing it from becoming overgrown.

There are three sleeping options, starting with the eponymous Kudhvas. Four of these geometric structures are built into the trees, two metres above the ground and accessible by ladder. Cleverly designed to span two floors, each one has a small double bed, a neat little sitting room and large glass windows which let the light pour in. The facilities may be basic, but the Kudhvas are brilliantly designed and truly unique.

Then there are two tipis, each of which comes complete with a large, comfortable double bed and jaw-dropping views over the coastline. Although perhaps the least unique type of accommodation on offer here, they're probably the best choice for those wanting a restful night's kip – the bed is larger than the other options, and there are no windows letting the light pour in early in the morning.

Finally, set apart from the heart of the Kudhva camp, at the top of a natural waterfall, is the Danish Cabin. It's an exceptional piece of architecture, and a great option for groups; it can sleep up to six, with two bunk beds and two pull-out beds. The cabin's beautifully designed interior is matched by its ingeniously engineered structure – its arrangement of folding walls allows you to transform the space from a cosy, enclosed sitting room to an open-air bar and kitchen area. Trees wrap around the building, blending it seamlessly into the surrounding forest, and the power for the cabin's lights is generated by the waterfall.

Whichever option you choose, you'll have full access to the site's facilities. You can cook up alfresco feasts on your fire pit in the Danish Cabin, or on a small open fire by your tipi or Kudhva; watch the sunset from the wood-fired hot tub; swim in the lake at the base of the quarry; or take part in sunset yoga by the old mill. Staying here is an immersive experience, the 'world' that Louise and her team have created transporting you a million miles from your day to day. A weekend at Kudhva helps you reconnect with nature, and reminds you to focus on life's smaller details.

If you're able to stay for longer, you can take advantage of the many other things to do and see in north Cornwall – several of which are in this book. We recommend hiking through the enchanted forest of St Nectan's Glen, exploring hidden beaches at low tide, swimming in the Bude sea pool, or soaking up the history of Tintagel Castle with its legendary links to King Arthur.

Don't forget

Pack your swimming stuff – a dip in the quarry's small lake followed by a soothing soak in a wood-fired hot tub is a must. If you're sensitive to light, or just want a lie-in, be sure to bring an eye mask; the Kudhvas are designed to let the natural light in so you wake and sleep with the sun. We loved this, but it's definitely not for everyone!

Wandering the desert of Dungeness

On England's far southeastern coast, Dungeness offers one of the most unique landscapes in the UK. Desolate, barren and strangely beautiful, it is often referred to as Britain's only desert, and it's not exactly hard to see why. As one of the largest expanses of shingle beach in Europe, this corner of the Kent coast is unlike any other.

Time	few hours
Fitness	low
Cost	free
Effort	low
Equipment	none
Transport	public transport available

Is this for me?

Located only a couple of hours' drive from the capital, Dungeness offers a very memorable experience due to its sheer otherworldly nature.

The pale, open shingle landscape is peppered with weathered huts, wild sea kale and abandoned fishing boats. It is also home to several lighthouses, two power stations and a small, functioning railway. Walking across this strange corner of Kent you can't help but feel inspired by its strange combination of nature, artistic expression and industrial heritage.

Though it's easy to spend longer here, you can get a good sense of Dungeness' eerie beauty in an hour or so, making it a good option even if you're short on time.

The adventure

Located between Folkestone and Hastings, at the foot of Romney Marsh, Dungeness is perched on a protruding section of the Kent coastline overlooking the English Channel. Getting there is fairly straightforward; a two-hour drive south for those living in the capital and for those without a car, there are also buses from the nearby train stations at Rye, Ashford and Folkestone.

On arrival, you'll quickly grasp the pure bizarreness of Dungeness. But please, don't perceive this strangeness as a negative. For us it was very much a positive, a sort of epic oddness that you would be more likely to experience in a remote corner of Texas than on England's south coast.

Your sense of scale is immediately skewed by the huge power station looming over small weather-beaten huts, upturned boats and driftwood sculptures. The stripped-back colours of the landscape almost make it feel like a painting, with the wide open sky, the sea of shingle and the waters of the Channel, all in varying shades of blue and grey. The only interruptions are the salt-crusted browns and blacks of the buildings, and the muted greens of the hardy, wind-tossed plants. This artistic oddness has attracted all kinds of creatives over the years, most famously Derek Jarman, whose beautiful home and lovingly designed shingle garden at Prospect Cottage are still here (visit by timed ticket only).

This feeling of creativity infuses Dungeness, and you'll find it impossible to ignore as you weave your way around the coast. The huts with their beautifully faded colours; the lighthouses with Wes Anderson-like symmetry; the hundreds of small sculptures... It feels like you've stepped into a large-scale art installation, one that immediately makes you feel smaller and less important. Perhaps this is where Dungeness' real sense of adventure lies. It almost feels as if you've slipped into a parallel world, one which encourages you to more freely explore your own artistic side.

This certainly isn't an adventure in the conventional sense – there's no hiking up mountainsides or tackling raging rapids. But therein lies its beauty. Adventure should take you somewhere new, not only physically but also in terms of your internal experience, and Dungeness is guaranteed to deliver on that.

Activities

If you would like to extend your time in Dungeness, here are three activities we highly recommend:

Royal Society for the Protection of Birds (RSPB) Dungeness

Dungeness is home to the RSPB's oldest nature reserve, which sprawls over 1000 hectares of Romney Marsh. This Site of Special Scientific Interest is great to visit all year round, and has four trails and a multitude of lookouts, hides and viewpoints from which to watch the wildlife.

Romney, Hythe and Dymchurch Railway

The RH&DR is a light locomotive railway that runs between Hythe and Dungeness, taking you up close to the nuclear power stations and lighthouse. Riding on a heritage locomotive as it chugs across the shingle makes a great and typically bizarre addition to your experience.

Old Lighthouse

This imposing 46-metre high and 11-metre wide lighthouse dates back to 1904, and is now Grade II listed. You can buy tickets to look around the extraordinary structure, but be sure to check their website in advance as opening times are irregular and subject to change.

Don't forget

People actually live here, so please respect that fact and don't go snooping too close to the houses. You can definitely enjoy Dungeness without encroaching on private spaces.

A weekend on Dartmoor

Time	multi-day
Fitness	medium
Cost	affordable
Effort	medium
Equipment	none
Transport	best by car

With its ponies roaming free across craggy landscapes, ancient wooded valleys, an intricate network of rivers and remarkable tors, Dartmoor is a place like no other. A day spent exploring this magical landscape can be jam-packed with as many adventurous activities as your appetite can handle. It offers the perfect example of the Great British outdoors, and is a must-visit for anyone searching for adventure.

Is this for me?

Dartmoor offers a varied menu of activities, with bike trails, incredible hiking, fantastic pubs, outdoor swimming spots and the possibility of wild camping. The only real challenge is getting there. Exeter is the nearest major city, and the public transport links – trains between Exeter and Okehampton, plus some largely seasonal bus services – aren't the most extensive.

The adventure

Dartmoor National Park is a vast expanse of moorland in the south of Devon, often touted as one of the last truly wild parts of England.

Once here, you are spoilt for choice, as there are so many activities to fill a weekend. We have been lucky enough to visit the park several times, and now have some firm favourites.

First up is Wistman's Wood, one of the most magical places in the whole of the UK. Said to be what's left of a prehistoric forest that once covered much of Dartmoor, this small wood is made up of stunted oak trees covered in thick moss, which entwine to form a ceiling of green, while rocks coated in lichens fuse to create a living carpet. Stepping into the woods, it's hard to believe you haven't been transported into some sort of ancient fairytale.

The inspiration for countless poems and paintings, the woods are a world unto themselves, and although small they're easy to get lost in. A trip here will remind you just how incredible nature can be.

One of the National Park's most famous sights isn't a location at all, though. It's home to around 1500 Dartmoor ponies, hardy animals which graze on wild grasses and huddle together in the winter. They're usually not hard to find, roaming free over the moors, and in the spring months you may well get lucky and catch a glimpse of the newborn foals.

Dartmoor is also home to an intricate and beautiful network of rivers, providing plenty of opportunities for an invigorating wild swim. From the pools at Poundsgate to the natural water slides near Oakham, Dartmoor certainly provides for those looking for the revitalizing benefits of a swim in nature. Whether you want to cool down in the summer months or wake up with an icy winter plunge, a trip to Dartmoor isn't truly complete without a dip.

But topping the list of Dartmoor's must-try activities is a hike to the tors. About the only things interrupting the vast and open scrub-covered moorland, these towers of rock are a product of years of weathering. Over time the landscape has worn away to reveal jutting chunks of granite, which have then slowly eroded into often strange and precarious-looking shapes.

Exploring between the tors feels a little like discovering a prehistoric world, with the natural statues scattered seemingly at random across the landscape, creating a bizarre sight. The park is home to over 160 tors, ranging from small and accessible to remote and towering, so you're spoilt for choice.

Eating and drinking

Riverford Field Kitchen

If you're after fresh food, then Riverford is just the place. Their Field Kitchen serves seasonal, organic dishes made with vegetables and herbs grown on their farm and in their kitchen garden just metres from the restaurant. This multi-award-winning kitchen prides itself on providing guests with an experience to remember. With no starters or mains, the vegetable-focused dishes instead arrive at your table in one long flow of deliciousness to share with your family and friends.

Northmore Arms

Now this is a proper pub! Hidden away along the high-hedgerowed lanes of Dartmoor, a polite sign on the door of the Northmore Arms states 'No mobile phones', setting the tone for what is a truly traditional watering hole. Small with low ceilings, a large fireplace and decades of local memorabilia decorating the walls, it is everything you want in a countryside pub. If you're after food, be sure to book ahead – it really is a snug pub, and fills up fast.

Don't forget

The weather on Dartmoor can be unpredictable, so bring waterproof layers. Also, some parts of northern Dartmoor are used by the army as a firing range. You can check the times online for scheduled dates, but if you see a red flag or lamp while walking in this section of the moor, turn around – that means there could be live firing happening.

A sunrise swim in the River Thames

Starting the day with a pre-breakfast cold-water swim is a game-changer. It knocks any grogginess out of your system and sets you up for the day ahead – as well as giving you a chance to connect with nature before settling into your usual routine. It's amazing what you can achieve before 9am with a bit of pre-planning and alarm setting!

Time	few hours
Fitness	medium
Cost	free
Effort	medium
Equipment	none
Transport	best by car

Is this for me?

If you are looking for a quick, free adventure, this adventure is for you. What's more, you could even fit this one in before you clock on for the day! And if you have more time, you can of course extend your trip along the river. As long as you can swim and don't mind getting out of bed fairly early, then this is a very straightforward adventure.

It's also an adaptable adventure. While the exact spot we chose is only accessible by car, there are plenty of other places you can reach on public transport.

The adventure

Before we start, it's important to state that this adventure is more of a template than anything – we know that not everybody will be within an hour of this spot. Think of it as a sample of what you can do along the Thames, and even if you're nowhere near this particular river, we hope it can inspire you to find some places near your own home for a refreshing pre-work swim – it really is a great feeling!

This adventure is best enjoyed on a warm summer's day and, if possible, you should be rising before the sun does. You know how it goes... You go to sleep full of enthusiasm and good intentions, but when the alarm goes off that thought hits you: is this going to be worth it? Well in our experience, it absolutely is. Resist the temptation to hit snooze, and choose to start your day in an adventurous way. Make your early start easier by preparing your breakfast supplies (we brought along a camping stove) and swimming gear the night before – trust us on that one.

When most people think of the River Thames they think of the vast waterway flowing through central London. But all rivers start somewhere! In the case of the Thames, its humble beginnings are close to Lechlade, a leafy Gloucestershire village. The Thames is idyllic here, meandering through the countryside surrounded by green and wildlife. This stretch of the river is also great if you're into history, with a string of WWII pillboxes embedded in the embankment.

Using Google Earth, we zoomed in around this area and found what looked like a great swimming spot southeast of Lechlade, on a bend that also housed a pillbox. There are several pillboxes along this relatively short stretch of river; they tend to be on the northern bank, while the easiest places to park are on the southern one, leaving you with a fun challenge if you want to get your breakfast supplies across the river! Our solution was to take a tight-sealed plastic storage box, fill it with our gear and swim across with it. This worked extremely efficiently as it basically floated, and when we reached the other side everything was bone dry. Stage one complete.

Once we had reached the other side we dropped our stuff off, found an opening and jumped back into the water. There is something joyously free about leaping into a wild river as the sun comes up on a summer's morning. We floated on our backs as the current took us slowly round the bend, where we got out, ran back round the meander and started again. One of the purest forms of fun.

After 45 minutes of frolicking like kids we dried off and helped each other up onto the top of a pillbox, hauling our supplies with us. From that higher vantage point we were able to see our surroundings in more detail. By then it was a glorious morning, and we set about scoffing our breakfast as the sun warmed us up.

Once we were full, we simply climbed down and swam across the river again. Back on the other side, we dried off, jumped back in the car and cracked on with our day. It couldn't be simpler.

Starting the day like this is incredible. It highlights how much you can get done before the work day has even started, and is the perfect way to add some adventure into your week. I'm not sure we can recommend it any more than we already have!

Don't forget

Unfortunately, the rise in open-water swimming here in the UK has led to an increase in drownings. No matter what you do, be careful! Do your research on where you plan to swim, don't go alone and don't get into water that you might not be able to handle.

Sewage and pollution have also been an issue due to policy changes in recent years, and certain areas have become unswimmable. You can download the Safe Seas and Rivers Service app to check water quality before settling on a spot.

Hiking the St Nectan's Glen loop

Hidden in the depths of Cornwall is one of the UK's only temperate rainforests. It's a magical place that ancient legend suggests is the veil between our world and the underworld. Local tales say fairies, pixies and nymphs make their homes here. Whether you buy into these Celtic stories or not, the charm and allure of the glen is obvious, especially with the 18-metre waterfall cascading through the rocks hidden away at one end.

Time few hours

Fitness medium

Cost affordable

Effort medium

Equipment none

Transport best by car

Is this for me?

Due to its relatively remote location this adventure has fairly poor public transport links, so it's best tackled by car. Once you're there, though, you will be rewarded for your efforts with a four-mile loop walk over pretty flat and easy terrain, suitable for people of most ages and abilities.

This adventure isn't heavy on the adrenaline, but what it lacks in high-octane thrills it more than makes up for in natural wonder. The loop leads you through the thick green fauna of St Nectan's Glen, past the waterfall, before leading you out along the dramatic coast where you can climb down to the beaches for a dip in the ocean.

The adventure

The ancient woodland of St Nectan's Glen is located near Trethevy, a small village northeast of Tintagel in north Cornwall. There are several different routes that loop through the glen and back to the coast in this area; we've outlined one that we thought worked really well below.

Put the Bossiney Cove carpark into your navigation app and head there. Then use it to guide you through a small holiday park and along clearly marked public footpaths through a few fields. This first section will take around 20 minutes before landing you at a gate to the glen.

You won't struggle to know once you've reached it. One moment you are in ordinary farmland, then one gate later you are walking through a tunnel of green – it's like you've stepped into a Tolkien novel. From there the trail becomes even more obvious,

61

the well-marked track leading you through the thick forest, across a series of wooden bridges and towards the most inland section of the glen.

At the far end of the glen is St Nectan's Kieve, which you enter through a café (you'll need to pay a small fee). Kieve is Cornish for basin, and refers to the pool at the foot of the waterfall which is the undoubted star of this remarkable forest. It's an 18-metre drop down mossy stone, passing through a hole in the rock face just before it meets the basin.

As you stand there somewhat entranced, you'll notice dozens of colourful ribbons tied to branches and hung from the rocks. These are wishing ribbons, left by those who believe in this spot's magical healing powers.

The second half of the adventure takes you along some country lanes back through the valley in which the glen sits. From here the path will lead you out of the thick green of the forest to follow the River Trevillet until it reaches the coast. Here, the valley opens up to reveal a series of rugged, rocky coves. This is Bossiney Haven, a small secluded spot perfect for a post-hike dip. The path down is steep and rocky, but it's well worth it for the gold-sand beach revealed when the tide is out.

Finally, from here a small track leads you back from the coast to the carpark, completing the loop.

Don't forget

As mentioned, to see the waterfall you will need to pay a fee. The fee will be put towards protecting and maintaining the area for future generations. What's more, the access it gives you is certainly worth the money.

Of course, you'll need to pack a swimming costume. There's no reason not to swim at Bossiney, since you'll be walking there anyway!

Located between the coasts of Devon and Wales, Lundy is the largest island in the Bristol Channel. The clear waters surrounding the island, protected as the UK's first Marine Conservation Zone, are home to over 200 grey seals – so if you've dreamed of swimming with them, this is the place to go.

Time full day

Fitness medium

Cost affordable

Effort medium

Equipment none

Transport public transport available

Devon, England

Snorkelling with seals off Lundy Island

Is this for me?

If you suffer from seasickness then perhaps you should give this one a miss, as getting here requires a couple of hours on a small boat each way. If you've got solid sea legs, and you enjoy discovering lesser-visited corners of the UK, then you will most likely enjoy this adventure.

What's more, there are fairly good transport links for those without a car. Ilfracombe even boasts a direct National Express bus from London Victoria.

The adventure

The vast majority of boat charters start from Ilfracombe, a picturesque seaside town on the north Devon coast. Before you do anything else, book with one of the operators based in the harbour there, of which there are several. Be warned: the boats get booked up really quickly in the summer.

The day trips to Lundy take around eight to ten hours in total, so make sure you take lots of water, sun cream and any other supplies you may want. If you are planning on setting foot on the island, note that its one pub is the only place you'll be able to get food or drink, so bring snacks!

In terms of sea-based activities once you get to the island, you have the choice to either snorkel or dive. We weren't qualified to dive, so we chose to snorkel, but Lundy is home to some of the best dive waters in the UK. There is an abundance of sea life around here, as well as several wrecks, attracting many keen divers from around the world. You can get wetsuit, mask and snorkel hire as part of the package when chartering a boat, but you'll need your own kit for diving.

The time will fly by as you cross to the island, the beautiful north Devon coastline growing ever more distant behind you. If you're lucky, you may spot the local pod of dolphins on your way. The boat will eventually drop anchor in a small bay on the east of Lundy, where you'll get your first chance to get in the water.

You'll see seals almost immediately, as they're very inquisitive and will most likely swim up to the boat. They're hard to miss!

After a couple of hours your skipper will give you the opportunity to spend some time on the island, an option we recommend taking. A long concrete path cuts through the cliff line and winds up onto the top of the island. From here you can get a real sense of the place for the first time. About three miles (five km) long and just over half a mile (0.8 km) wide, Lundy is completely car-free. You can walk the entire island within a couple of hours.

The island is home to two disused lighthouses, the fantastic Marisco Tavern pub and of course plenty of gorgeous flora and fauna. We highly recommend climbing the Old Light, with its immense views over the island and sea, before

stopping for lunch. The pub was built in the 1860s, and its vaulted wooden ceilings and maritime memorabilia speak to its long history.

Before you know it, it will be time to head down to the boat and back to mainland Devon. But if one day isn't enough to take in the beauty of this special little island, why not stay the night? There are 23 self-catering properties available to stay in, and for such a tiny place the range is impressive. Take your pick from a thirteenth-century castle, a simple fisherman's cottage, a renovated Georgian villa and even an old lighthouse. For those wanting something a little lighter on the wallet, there is also a campsite on the island.

Don't forget

If you're planning to stay overnight, book early. By the time we looked everything had already been snapped up.

67

Hike up into the mountains at the heart of the Lake District National Park in search of this hidden treasure. Find it, and you'll be rewarded with one of the best windows you'll ever look out of, perfectly framing a spectacular view across the valley towards Buttermere and Crummock Water. A truly unforgettable spot.

Time few hours

Fitness medium

Cost free

Effort medium

Equipment some recommended

Transport public transport available

Cumbria, England

Taking in the view from Warnscale Bothy

Is this for me?

Though the bothy itself is well hidden, the area in general is one of the easier places to reach ◆ in the heights of the Lake District. There's a convenient carpark only about an hour's walk from the bothy itself. That said, this isn't the easiest walk as you'll be tackling steep slopes and uneven terrain. If you feel fit enough to handle it, you really should go. It is absolutely one of England's most extraordinary views.

At its simplest, this adventure can stop at a short hike. That's a little bit of a waste, though – if you're visiting a bothy, you should definitely stay there if you have the time.

The adventure

Warnscale is a small bothy set up in the mountains of the Lake District. You'll be hard-pressed to find it; almost the entire building is made from slate, and set as it is on a rocky slate slope, it blends seamlessly into the surrounding landscape. Catch it at the wrong angle, and it's perfectly camouflaged.

The locals call Warnscale 'a room with a view' – and it really is! The one-room bothy looks over Lake Buttermere and Crummock Water, the one window framing the view like a postcard.

Preparing ahead of your trip is important here. The bothy is remote, so you won't be able to get any supplies once you're there. If you are planning on staying the night then you will also need to bring sleeping mats and sleeping bags to lay on the stone beds, and fire-making supplies. Bring plenty of layers too.

The adventure starts at Honister Pass carpark, linked by bus to nearby towns. From there, begin the 1.3-mile (2-km) hike up into the barren landscape.

> **Tip: Be sure to check the weather before you set off. The conditions are very harsh, and can turn on you without warning. We did this hike in March, and the navigation was especially difficult for us, due to the fog hiding the lie of the land. Despite it all, we enjoyed the extra challenge, and it made reaching the bothy all the more rewarding.**

Take the route that's signposted 'Haystacks'. This will lead you along the first and steepest section of the trail. After the path flattens out you'll have to hike for another 15 minutes to reach Dubs Hut. This bothy is a great waypoint to know you're on the right trail. By this time you will be really in the depths of this harsh corner of the Lake District, with nothing but rock-strewn views in every direction. To your left you will see a small river interrupting the rocks; head down the slope along a faint trail and cross the river, using whichever stepping stones you deem safest.

After you rejoin the path on the other side of the water, you will need to keep your eyes peeled for Warnscale. And I mean really peeled. It's just around the corner, but very much hidden in plain sight. It took us a little while to locate it, but we found it in the end. The telltale chimney stood out from the surrounding mountains, which was enough for us to see it. It's really quite something how much it blends in!

Once you've found it, you'll get your reward. Step through the front door and you'll catch a glimpse through the window. The harsh environment you've been hiking through suddenly transforms into a painting, with the grey tones making way for steep-sided green mountains and sweeping views down to the vast lakes in the valley below.

Don't forget

Staying here is first come, first served, so you are not guaranteed a bed. We were planning on stopping overnight, but arrived to find two groups of people already there. The bothy code (page 223) prohibits too large a number staying, so we couldn't join them. Be prepared for this eventuality by leaving enough time to get back to your car in daylight.

If you do stay, leave the bothy clean and tidy for the next visitors. It's also common to leave some non-perishable supplies; matches and playing cards go down particularly well. It's this type of community-focused behaviour that keeps the bothying system going!

A winter sunset over Holkham Nature Reserve

Settle down on the sand dunes to watch thousands of birds flock through the skies of the Holkham Nature Reserve. Enjoy a brief walk before choosing a comfy spot from which to watch the sun setting over the Norfolk countryside. This is UK adventure at its most peaceful, making for a restorative after-work trip, or a weekend winter getaway.

Time few hours

Fitness low

Cost free

Effort low

Equipment none

Transport best by car

Is this for me?

Norfolk can seem pretty isolated from the rest of the UK, which may be why it sees fewer tourists than its neighbours. If you're willing to make the effort to get there, you'll be rewarded with stunning and uncrowded landscapes, especially in winter. Once you make it to the Holkham area, this adventure is super-achievable, quick and easy.

The adventure

Depending on where you're based, if you tackle this adventure in summer you could make it in time for sunset after work. However, we strongly suggest you head out to the reserve in winter, even if that means nudging the trip into the weekend instead. Holkham is a perfect example of how beautiful England can be in the colder months.

This leads us nicely to preparations. No matter what time of year you head this way, you will want to take plenty of supplies. In the winter months the key is warmth: bring cosy clothes, a rug for sitting on the dunes and a thermos of something hot at least. We'd also suggest packing a picnic, as this is a great place to eat alfresco. The nearby town of Burnham Market has a few nice places to grab food, like the Tuscan Farm Shop where you can get lots of posh picnic bits and bobs.

To get there, don't put Holkham National Nature Reserve into your navigation app as it will likely take you to the main carpark. Instead put in 'Burnham Overy Staithe', a picturesque seaside village that gives you access to what is, in our opinion, the most beautiful and varied part of the reserve.

There is a carpark on the beach in Burnham Overy Staithe, from where a raised walking path heads out towards the coast. Follow it, and watch as the unique drama of the area slowly unfolds around you. The veins of the tidal backwaters and reed-strewn beginnings of the wetlands are simply magical.

It won't take long for you to feel gloriously isolated, and fully immersed in nature. It will only take you about 20 minutes to reach the far western end of Holkham Beach, with its series of gorgeous undulating dunes. Once here, you just need to choose a winner – which dune delivers on the brief of height combined with comfort? Take your pick, then head to the top and just look around. There is something different in every direction: the slate-grey North Sea in front of you; Scolt's Head tidal island along the coast to your left; and to your right, pine forests running into the sand. Last of all, look behind you towards the wetlands – that's where the real magic happens.

Set up camp on your dune of choice, tuck into your picnic if you've brought one, and settle in for the show. Come dusk, thousands of birds gather in flocks, dancing across the skyline. Twisting and turning, they form mesmerizing shapes against the pink backdrop as they swoop back and forth. Shore larks, sparrowhawks, twites, geese and many, many more fill the colourful skies, which reflect in the water below.

As the light begins to fade it's time to return to the car, so make sure you allow yourself enough time to get back safely. There are plenty of local pubs where you can warm up post-expedition, should you fancy. The closest is The Nelson, with the Hoste Arms in Burnham Market another good option.

Don't forget

Be very wary of the weather! In the winter, you are likely to get stuck in the harsh wind and rain. You should keep an eye on the weather before you commit to travelling, as the experience really depends on a good sunset.

Canoeing the River Thames

A challenging but rewarding 140-mile (225-km) canoe trip along the UK's most famous river. This adventure will completely change your perception of the Thames, and show you some of what this picturesque and varied part of England really has to offer.

Time multi-day

Fitness high

Cost affordable

Effort high

Equipment required

Transport best by car

Is this for me?

This is, without a doubt, the hardest adventure in this book. You will be challenged physically, emotionally and logistically. It will test your patience, your endurance and your taste for adventure. That said, for every moment of discomfort and pain, the reward is tenfold. If you are seeking an incomparable experience, this is the trip for you.

Over 140 miles (225 km) is one hell of a trip for anyone, so if you don't fancy doing the whole thing, then we highly recommend just getting out on the water and doing some of it. There are many amazing sections on this route, so feel free to pick and choose which ones suit you the most. Go for one of the shorter ones, and you could even fit it into an afternoon.

The adventure

The most famous part of the River Thames is undoubtedly its final section, which snakes its way through central London flanked by high-rise buildings. This enormous body of water releases an Olympic swimming pool of water into the sea every 40 seconds – but you wouldn't know that if you headed upstream. Before the water passes through the buzz of the capital it has already been on quite the journey, beginning life as just a trickle in the much calmer, rural setting of Thames Head, Gloucestershire.

For the sake of this chapter, we will outline the route that we took over eight days. It stretches from Lechlade (the earliest point where the river is deep enough for a canoe), through to where it becomes tidal at Teddington Lock.

Day 1: Lechlade to Eynsham Lock

Lechlade is a town of about 2500 people right on the southern edge of the Cotswolds. It's a beautiful place to start your adventure, as you paddle round the overgrown green meanders, taking in this quintessentially English section of the route. We made the most of it by scheduling breaks to stop and swim (see page 57) where it was especially beautiful.

As the day comes to an end, pull up at Eynsham Lock and rest your tired limbs. Eynsham Lock Campsite is a good cheap option, but isn't open year round. There is also Oxford Riverside Glamping here, a more luxurious option with pre-erected tents and proper beds.

> **Tip: Lechlade has some places where you can stock up for this adventure if needed. The whole route passes through plenty of towns, villages and even cities, so you'll have ample opportunity to restock along the way.**

Day 2: Eynsham Lock to Clifton Hampden

The start of this section is blissful, with yet more gentle bends in the river leading you to Oxford's Port Meadow. In springtime, you will find it carpeted with buttercups, with cows grazing and many varieties of birds taking to the water. Settle here for a picnic breakfast or brunch on the banks, idyllic on a sunny day.

The second half of the day brings a change of pace. The rural waterway turns urban, heading through the centre of this bustling university city. Take in views of landmarks from river level as you push to make it to Clifton Hampden, where there's a riverside campsite. It's definitely worth doing to avoid getting stuck in Oxford!

> **Tip: Do you want to do the full length of the river but at a more relaxed pace? Make an extra day in your schedule and split the first two days into three. These are the longest and most challenging sections, and we would have split them up further if we had the time.**

Day 3: Clifton Hampden to Goring Lock

After the first two days of exertion, you'll start day three feeling sore and tired. However, you can keep yourself distracted by daydreaming about which of the incredible houses and estates lining the river you might buy when that big lottery win finally comes in. So impressive are the houses that, before you know it, you'll be drifting into Goring Lock where you'll dock your canoe and spend the night.

At this point, if you're like us, you may well be in real need of a comfy bed and wholesome grub. There are a couple of nice pubs located close to the river here, which are good options for both food and accommodation.

Day 4: Goring Lock to Shiplake

Day four takes you along another urban section of the river, this time through Reading. A darling of music lovers across the UK, the city will make for a noteworthy change of pace as you paddle through. It is quite different from the trip so far, but that isn't a bad thing!

As you make your way northeast of the city you'll reach Shiplake, where the city scenes fade and you get back to paddling through gorgeous open countryside. There is a collection of small islands here, which we recommend stopping at to check out. Set up camp here and enjoy a soothing evening swim in the calm waters. Some people even spend the night, but do be sure to check local guidelines before pitching up. Either way, this is a gorgeous place to spend the evening.

Day 5: Shiplake to Cookham

A glorious morning of paddling past field-lined riverbanks in this agricultural artery of the UK. Before long you will reach Henley-on-Thames' pristine stretch of river, before continuing on to the historic riverside town of Cookham. Here there are several lovely pubs where you can stop for a restorative pint. Our favourite is the Bel and The Dragon, which dates back to 1417, making it one of the oldest licensed houses in England. This is also a great accommodation option if you're feeling in need of a comfy bed for the night.

Day 6: Cookham to Old Windsor

By this point, the river no longer feels remote and rural. Instead, it's teeming with life – you'll cross paths with boaters, kayakers, paddle boarders and walkers. They're all here for the same reason as you: to make the most of the Thames. If you're looking for a lively, convivial atmosphere, this is a good section for you.

If you fancy one last night under the stars, then this could be the place for it. While there is no official campsite, we contacted a local horse sanctuary and asked if we could camp on their land if we gave a donation, and they happily agreed.

Day 7: Old Windsor to Sunbury

The capital is coming. You can feel the buzz of the big smoke from miles away, the noise and energy of the capital becoming more noticeable as you pull closer to its outer suburbs. It's an exciting change from earlier parts of the adventure, but not the most peaceful section to choose if you're only looking to do a day.

Still, the convenience if you're coming from London is also very desirable. And if you enjoy sightseeing, famous landmarks like Hampton Court Palace make it worthwhile.

When it comes to where to settle down for the night, The Flower Pot and The Weir Hotel are both good options. They're conveniently situated on the river, so you can hop out of the boat and relax with little faff.

Day 8: Sunbury to Teddington Lock

This is the shortest section of the whole trip. This final paddle takes you from Sunbury all the way to Teddington Lock. You'll travel through Kingston, a popular suburb in the southwest of London. Teddington is just around the corner, and with it the Tide End pub. Stop here for a well-deserved victory pint and a slap-up meal. You made it!

Don't forget

The weather definitely helped us in achieving this adventure, so we'd recommend you attempt it in the warmer, drier months too. This means you'll need sunscreen and lots of water. It may sound obvious, but you'd be surprised how easy it is to forget – we've learned the hard way!

We underestimated the upper body strength and endurance required to tackle this adventure, and did it with zero training. Despite all odds, we still managed to do it, but we'd suggest you try a smaller canoeing trip first, or just a section of this one.

A stroll between the white rock stacks of Botany Bay pre-breakfast is the perfect way to start the day, no matter the time of year. Each season offers something different – a crisp, sunny winter's morning bathes the bay in a glorious golden light, while on a warm summer's day there's little excuse not to go for an invigorating dip in the Blue Flag-awarded waters (some of the cleanest in the UK).

Time	few hours
Fitness	low
Cost	free
Effort	low
Equipment	none
Transport	public transport available

Kent, England

Sunrise at Botany Bay

Is this for me?

At its simplest, this adventure is essentially a stroll along the beach. If you're looking for more, though, amp it up with a swim, kayak or some outdoor cooking. It is also very easy to get to, with a carpark and good public transport links. Due to its location and beauty, Botany Bay can get crowded, especially in the summer months. You can, however, avoid the crowds by setting your alarm for an early hour and getting down there at first light.

The adventure

A quick history lesson to kick this adventure off. Botany Bay found its name due to the smugglers who used to operate here in the 1700s. After their arrest, they were punished with hard labour in the Australian prison colony of, you guessed it, Botany Bay. Sure, it doesn't have the consistent temperatures of its Aussie counterpart, but it more than makes up for that with its stark white cliffs, chalk stacks, golden sands and rock pools.

Once you arrive at the beachfront carpark, either by car or on foot from the bus stop seven minutes away, head down the small slope to the sand, which stretches uninterrupted to the north. Go south and you'll find some quite beautiful rock stacks and, further along, a mass of pools revealed at low tide. It's a great place to search for sea life; you are likely to find crabs, starfish, and anemones. Keep going this way and you'll find yourself turning the corner through a natural tunnel, one of the most striking features of this coastline. This is a great little walk, especially at sunrise, when the soft light is bouncing off the white cliffs and stacks.

While there is plenty of sand even at high tide, low tide is, in our opinion, when Botany Bay really comes to life. As the water retreats it uncovers a whole new world; in the rock pools that form you will find crabs, shrimps, sea urchins and more hidden in the nooks and crannies. For those wanting a longer walk, an otherwise hidden path to nearby Joss Bay also emerges. Just make sure you time it properly!

Botany Bay is part of the North Foreland stretch of Kent chalk headland, and therefore is home to some great fossil hunting. It's one of the best beaches in the UK for unearthing 65-million-year-old treasures, so keep your eyes peeled. If you do spot any fossils embedded in the white cliffs, please do leave them where they are for safety reasons.

If you want to make your experience of Botany Bay a bit more active, we'd recommend renting a kayak to explore this stretch of coast from the water. Dipping in and out of the different coves gives you a whole new perspective on the dramatic white cliffs. Alternatively, you could hire a wetsuit and surfboard at Joss Bay and ride some waves.

You could also stop at Botany Bay as part of a longer walk, such as the Viking Coast Trail. This 32-mile (51-km) loop connects the bay to Margate, Broadstairs and Ramsgate, and the whole route is perfect for a multi-day hike or cycle excursion. If you want to explore on two wheels, we'd suggest either bringing your own bike or renting one; Margate Bikes & Hire shop is a good option.

Don't forget

Botany Bay is very close to Margate, so consider visiting the artsy seaside town while you're here. You'll find a fleet of incredible restaurants, bars and shops to explore, plus the Turner Contemporary gallery.

Waking up in the wilderness of Elmley, you are transported to a slower, calmer world, one where the pace is dictated by the native wildlife and swaying of the long grass. A trip here will refresh and reset you as you reconnect with the natural world. Stay overnight to really immerse yourself.

Time multi-day
Fitness low
Cost costly
Effort low
Equipment none
Transport best by car

Kent, England

A night at Elmley Nature Reserve

Is this for me?

If you are looking for an adventure close to London that forces you to slow down and appreciate the smaller details, then there aren't many options better than Elmley. Its real value comes from just being there, switching off and allowing nature's restorative powers to wash over you.

The adventure

In the southeast of the Isle of Sheppey is Elmley Nature Reserve, a 3300-acre expanse which is home to over 40 species of bird. The family-run site also has an array of beautifully designed accommodation options, ranging from basic shepherds' huts and bell tents through to the luxury of the Kingshill Farmhouse, which boasts five exquisitely designed rooms. No matter what level of comfort you decide to go for, one thing is for sure: you will be embedded deep in nature, and will feel much further away from city life than you actually are.

Elmley is conservation-led, with the family who own it committing to a long-term plan to rewild the area and restore its biodiversity. To really make the most of this during your stay, we recommend ditching your phone, setting your Out Of Office and just focusing on experiencing the incredible landscapes and wildlife you have on your doorstep. Poking your head out of the window in the morning can lead to all kinds of sightings, from brown hares to owls, wagtails and wildfowl. Elmley is, quite literally, alive and kicking.

If you're after a deeper dive into the natural wonders of the reserve, book onto one of the safari experiences, during which on-site experts lead you along the nature trails to learn more about the local wildlife.

The almost eerie size and flatness of Elmley creates a feeling so foreign to the density of the mainland that you will quite quickly forget your proximity to it. It is this sense of scale combined with the immediate and immersive connection with the outdoors that makes your time here so special.

Don't forget

Make sure to book in advance as Elmley is very popular and can get busy. Packing for a night here is straightforward, with all the essentials available on site – just be sure to bring some good walking boots.

Cornwall, England

Sunset at Gurnard's Head

On a clear evening there aren't many more dramatic places to watch the sunset over the ocean than Gurnard's Head. It juts out from an isolated peninsula at the mercy of the elements, into the choppy waters off Cornwall's north coast. Walking across the craggy cliffs and over the wide-open moorland of the Penwith Peninsula on a clear evening is an unforgettable taste of wild west Cornwall.

Time	few hours
Fitness	low
Cost	free
Effort	low
Equipment	none
Transport	best by car

Is this for me?

Situated near the furthest southern tip of mainland Britain, this spot isn't the easiest place to get to. That said, if you live, or are staying, in the area, it's well worth making your way here. The actual walk to the headland is a little rocky but straightforward, making it suitable for people of most mobility levels. You can also extend the walk to take you along the clifftops, which we recommend you do. At its most basic level, this adventure is an incredible walk with an ocean view that ends at a great little pub. What's not to like?

The adventure

Gurnard's Head is on the north coast of Cornwall's Penwith Peninsula. By far the easiest way to get there is by car, along the region's narrow, winding roads. Put 'The Gurnard's Head (pub)' into your navigation app when you start your travels. The pub is the most convenient place to park if you're planning to drop in after your walk; if not, keep an eye out for the obvious parking spots just off the road as you approach the area. You'll know when you've arrived, as the pub is a bright yellow building and has 'Gurnard's Head' written across it in big letters – impossible to miss! If you don't have access to a car, take the number 16 bus that runs all the way from Penzance to Gurnard's Head a couple of times an hour.

Once there, you simply need to follow the road round to the right of the pub on foot. You'll head through the small hamlet of Treen, after which the road comes to a stop and you continue left along a small, well-trodden path through fields towards the sea. About 10 minutes later, you'll find yourself looking out over a dramatic headland jutting out into the water: Gurnard's Head.

The name is meant to reflect the rocks' resemblance to the head of a gurnard fish. Not knowing what a gurnard fish is or what it looks like, we can't tell you whether it's accurate! What we can tell you, though, is that it's a striking spot with truly stunning views along the cove-studded coastline and out over the ocean.

It is certainly worth exploring the rocky terrain of the headland, but like most landmarks such as this, once you're on it you can't appreciate its full beauty! We recommend retracing your steps and heading west along the coastal path. After just a few hundred metres, you'll reach the next part of the coast that protrudes out into the sea. A short scramble across the rocky grassland will take you to a point with glorious views back over Gurnard's Head.

As there's a series of flat grassy shelves here, you're also somewhat sheltered from the wind, making it a comfy spot to kick back and watch as the sun dips down towards the uninterrupted expanse of the Celtic Sea. It is an absolute gem of a spot, which provided one of our favourite-ever sunset-watching experiences.

Once the sun has slipped below the horizon, it's time to head back inland – maybe to warm up at the pub...

Don't forget

If you are keen on rounding the adventure off with a meal at the pub, be sure to book ahead as it can get very busy.

While walking along the coast, be careful to watch your footing at all times – especially after sunset.

Campervanning in the Peak District

The Peak District is a prime example of England's classic beauty. Enjoy rolling green hills, picturesque villages and plenty of opportunities for adventure. This trip is best tackled in a campervan, with everything you need for the next few days in one place. And that extra level of comfort compared to a tent is nice to boot!

Time multi-day

Fitness medium

Cost affordable

Effort medium

Equipment some recommended

Transport car required

Is this for me?

The Peak District is the perfect location for people of all ages wanting to get outdoors. It offers something for everyone, whether it be paragliding or just a short hike. The access to nature makes this region a playground for adventure seekers.

The addition of a campervan rental might not be for everyone. But, if you are planning on being there for a couple of nights, it will likely save you money compared to hotels and B&Bs! And of course, it will give you the freedom to go wherever takes your fancy.

The adventure

First things first: if you are planning on renting a campervan, you must get this booked very early. There's a whole host of companies offering short-term camper rentals, including classic 'backpacker' style campers and bespoke van conversions alike! We opted for a modern, digital-first camper from VWFS Rent-a-Car.

Once you get going, you have over 540 square miles (2000 square km) of the Peak District to explore at your leisure. We're lucky enough to have been a couple of times, and definitely have a few favourite spots and activities.

Tip: You won't be short on choice when it comes to campsites in the Peak District. That said, we opted for something a little closer to 'wild camping' by finding landowners who rent out space in their fields. This ensures you stay away from the crowds and gives the experience a more authentic feel. Check out PitchUp and Nearly Wild Camping if you'd like to do the same.

Bamford Edge

You can get the lie of the land at Bamford Edge, a dramatic bit of rock that juts out over the village of Bamford and the River Derwent in Hope Valley. The route up to it is one of the best short walks in the whole of the Peaks, with an easy hike up and truly incredible views from the top. It's also linked via a circular walk to Stanage Edge, another gritstone escarpment, which was featured in the 2005 *Pride and Prejudice* film.

Mountain biking

The park is absolutely perfect for mountain biking. With an abundance of trails, hidden valleys and undulating bridleways, there is something for all abilities; some routes of note are the Ladybower Loop, Linnet Clough and Hope Valley.

Chrome Hill

Another iconic Peak District sight, Chrome Hill is about 45 minutes' drive southwest of Bamford Edge, next to Parkhouse Hill in the Upper Dove Valley. It also goes by the name Dragon's Back; to appreciate why it got that nickname, survey it from the top of Parkhouse Hill. There is a great five-mile (eight-km) hike that leads you up both, and delivers some of the very best views in the area.

Three Shire Head

Though most of the Peak District National Park is in Derbyshire, it does also cross into neighbouring counties. There's a particularly beautiful spot where Cheshire, Derbyshire and Staffordshire meet: Three Shire Head. You'll find some of the best swimming waters in the region here. With two waterfalls, easy access and waters deep enough to plunge into, this is the perfect place to cool down on a balmy summer's day.

Don't forget

There are rules prohibiting wild camping (including in a campervan) throughout most of the national park, so book a spot to park up in advance.

Exploring Tregardock at low tide

There is something special about Tregardock Beach. Perhaps it's the overgrown pathways you need to follow to get there, or the view from the cliffs above. Maybe it's the unusual rock-strewn sand, revealed each time the tide goes out. Most likely it is a combination of all of the above, coming together to make this one of our absolute favourite UK beaches.

Time few hours

Fitness medium

Cost free

Effort medium

Equipment none

Transport car required

Is this for me?

Despite its location on the notoriously hectic north Cornwall coastline, Tregardock is uniquely peaceful. This is due to the fact that it isn't the easiest spot to access; parking is a 15- to 20-minute walk from the beach along a steep path which ends with a short clamber over often slippery rocks. So if you are thinking of setting out on this adventure, don't expect to just park your car and start running along the sand – that isn't going to happen! Not only is finding the hidden beach part of the fun, but as with most of these harder-to-reach spots, the bounty upon arrival is more than worth the effort.

The adventure

Tregardock is non-existent at high tide, with the water lapping right up at the cliff line, so go at the wrong time and you'll be searching in vain for a beach which isn't there... At low tide, though, the water slips away to reveal a fairly large stretch of sand interrupted only by an array of strangely shaped rocks and tidal pools, which lend it real character. Therefore, the first step in this adventure is checking the tide times.

Tip: If you have some flexibility in when you visit Tregardock, try to pick a day when the tide will start coming back in as the afternoon wanes. Arrive at the beach just after high tide, and you'll be there for the show as the water slowly pulls back and reveals the rock-flecked sand. This approach will give you the maximum amount of time to enjoy the beach before the tide starts to come back in, too.

Having figured out when you're going, you'll next need to work out where. In such a heavily touristed area, Tregardock is one of the semi-secret spots beloved by the locals, and we don't want to spoil its magic by laying out exactly how to get there. In any case, for us part of the adventure was conducting our own research and figuring it out for ourselves. We were tipped off by a local, and still didn't find it the first time, but this made eventually getting there even more satisfying – look at it as a treasure hunt of sorts!

What we will tell you is that, after you've parked, you need to follow a thin pathway towards the coast. Eventually you will reach the edge of a cliff, overlooking the beach which – if you have taken our advice about timing your visit – will be slowly appearing as the waves subside. This is your sign to take the steps built into the rock face down to the waterline. If you're impatient, like us, then you can then wade through the shallows to the first patch of sand.

Walk to the far end of the beach and you'll find some gorgeously clear rock pools, just a short scramble up from the sand. This is a great place to settle down later in the day as you watch the sun dip over the ocean, before you make your way back up when the tide starts encroaching.

This is a really local spot, and can't cope with hordes of visitors. If you're going to take the time to find it, please make sure you treat it with the utmost respect. And of course, don't tell anyone else how to get there – they need to earn it, just like you did!

Don't forget

Make sure you know the tide times precisely. Getting down onto the beach at the right time is one thing, but making sure you are off it before the tide comes back in is quite another. Judge this wrong and you run the risk of being cut off, which could put you in real danger. You should also avoid surfing here unless you're experienced, and shouldn't swim – there are fierce rip currents and submerged rocks.

Scotland

Size 30,977 square miles
(80,231 sq km)

National parks 2 (covering
7.3% of land area)

**UNESCO World Heritage
Sites** 6

Highest peak Ben Nevis
(1345m)

Islands over 900
(118 inhabited)

Lochs over 30,000

Discovering the beaches of Harris

The Isle of Harris has beaches like nowhere else in the UK. When you think of vast sweeps of white sand, it's probably the Maldives or Hawaii which come to mind – not the Outer Hebrides! But as it turns out, you don't need to leave Britain to find somewhere just as beautiful – albeit with rather chillier waters... As it's so remote, you may well find yourself exploring this island paradise alone.

Time multi-day

Fitness medium

Cost free

Effort medium

Equipment none

Transport car required

Is this for me?

If you can stretch your time and budget, this is one of those adventures we'd strongly recommend you try. We believe every Brit should get the chance to visit the Outer Hebrides at least once in their lifetime. If you've grown bored of tame rambles through pruned, pastoral countryside, this is where you go to dial up the drama.

Of course, the wild appeal of the Isle of Harris is partly preserved by its remoteness. The distance from almost anywhere outside Scotland is tremendous. Even from England's most northerly town, Berwick, you're looking at a good nine hours by car and ferry. If you're up for the road trip and ferry ride, though, you absolutely must make the time for this adventure. There's great payoff for your effort, as the diversity of scenery and wildlife will make you feel like you're taking three holidays at once.

The adventure

The Outer Hebrides – also called Na h-Eileanan an Iar, or the Western Isles – form part of the Hebridean archipelago, off the Scottish mainland's northwestern coast. There are 15 inhabited islands in the group, with only 45,000 residents in total. The diverse charms of Harris in particular are born from its location. On the western coast, the Atlantic gales bring ashore with them large amounts of crushed shells forming vast, sweeping sandy beaches. In comparison, its eastern coast has no sandy beaches and is instead deeply indented with rocky coves and jagged cliffs, making for an equally stunning but quite different experience. If you find the time for this adventure, make sure to enjoy the whole island!

> **Tip: As reaching the Isle of Harris flight-free is quite an undertaking from most parts of the UK, why limit yourself to a one-stop trip? You can create a route which takes you through several national parks, exploring various wild corners of Britain on your way. The rugged, remote charm of the Isle of Harris is worth the pilgrimage – trust us.**

Despite often being referred to as the Isle of Harris, it isn't actually a whole island, but rather the southern part of the Isle of Lewis and Harris. Though the north of the island is well worth exploring (see page 147), Harris is better known than Lewis, largely due to its sensational beaches. The remoteness of the archipelago means the coastline is blissfully free from overdevelopment. In fact, the main visitors to the shore are cows, sheep and horses. The local crofters (farmers) let their animals graze freely, so if you're after a flawless shot of Scotland's famous cattle, incongruously grazing by a tropical-looking beach, bring your camera!

Once on the island – either arriving in Tarbert, Harris' ferry port, which connects to Uig in Skye, or driving from Stornoway in Lewis, which connects to Ullapool on the mainland – you'll find all of the sandy west-coast beaches are connected by a basic single-track road network. It's easy to navigate, but very slow. Still, you'll hardly want to speed past those views! Below are a few of our favourites.

Luskentyre

Luskentyre is regularly voted one of the best beaches in the world, and it lives up to the hype. To reach it, take yourself to the northwest end of Harris, then follow the signposted single-track road for two miles around the swooping bay. When you reach a dead end, you'll be at the carpark, from where you simply need to cross the nearby dunes to reach the three-mile beach.

From Luskentyre, you'll get unbelievable views over Scottish mountains to your right as you look out to sea, the island of Taransay in front of you, and then behind you the windswept sand dunes. The dunes are a magical place to sit down for a picnic – look out for the local white ponies while you eat.

Seilebost Beach

Just a 15-minute drive south around the bay is Seilebost Beach. Seilebost boasts impressive views of the mountains of Ben Luskentyre and Taransay.

Take it slow and rest for a couple of days at the small campsite above the beach. For parking, follow signs to the Seilebost School West Harris Trust Campground, and once you're there, park against the roadside. Seilebost is a great spot to take a dip, so don't forget your swimmers and a towel.

Scarista

About 15 minutes' drive further south is Scarista Beach. If it weren't so close to Luskentyre, you would see pictures of it everywhere. It is an extraordinary beach in southwestern Harris, where a long stretch of white sand once again meets crystal-clear water framed by panoramic views over the Atlantic. Situated on the opposite side of Taransay to Luskentyre, this is a great beach for wildlife watching. Deer, seals and eagles have all been spotted here and wildflower meadows begin where the sand ends, meaning there is a lot to take in and enjoy. In summer, basking sharks have been known to pass through the Sound of Taransay, the stretch of sea between Taransay and Harris.

To access the beach, just head to the southern end of the small village of Scarista and park on the verge by a metal gate. From here, follow the path across the fields until you hit sand. At low tide on a calm day, Scarista is a beautiful swimming spot – but only for strong swimmers, as it can have powerful undercurrents. With long, repetitive waves due to the deep shelf, it is also popular with surfers. Bring your own board (or rent one from Surf Lewis and Harris in Sandwick near Stornoway), as you're out in the wild here and there is no handy rental shop on the edge of the beach.

Don't forget

Pack midge spray. You are a rare treat for these pesky bugs, so be prepared to spray often and spray well! The summer especially comes with the risk of midges ruining your day, so bring plenty of supplies to keep them at a respectful distance!

Along with bug spray, you'll need to bring all your rations and supplies from the mainland. There are only a few small shops on the island, with limited opening hours, so stop at the Co-op in Uig (where the ferry leaves the mainland for Harris) to stock up.

To put it simply, Stac Pollaidh is our favourite mountain in the UK. It has an unmistakable character, punctuated by its two rocky summits connected by a spectacular ridge. What's more, the views of the surrounding Assynt landscapes are some of the very best in Scotland, with miles upon miles of untamed nature in every direction.

Time	few hours
Fitness	medium
Cost	free
Effort	medium
Equipment	none
Transport	best by car

The Highlands, Scotland

Climbing Stac Pollaidh

Is this for me?

This short mountain climb has an incredible effort to reward ratio, with a short, sharp ascent resulting in views so extraordinary no language can do them justice. You just have to see them with your own eyes! It is a suitable climb for people of all ages, taking only an hour if you're fairly fit. Note that the so-called 'second summit' requires a bit of scrambling, so it isn't for everyone.

This adventure can be tackled all year round, but our preference would be autumn, just as the leaves are starting to turn.

The adventure

Stac Pollaidh, or Stac Polly for short, is located about half an hour's drive from Ullapool in the northwest Highlands, making it a great stop on the NC500 (see page 123) or a memorable day trip if you're staying nearby. Due to its remoteness, the best way to access Stac Polly is by car. The number 811 bus does link it to Ullapool, but the service is fairly infrequent so you'll need to check the timetable thoroughly.

The main route up starts from the carpark at the foot of the mountain. In peak season this can get full quickly, so you may have to find somewhere else to park up along the road. The best way to avoid this busy period is to get up at the crack of dawn and head there early. This way you will not only get a parking spot but also, far more excitingly, you will be able enjoy the spectacular morning light.

From the carpark, you cross the road and follow the path north up some steep steps and through a gate. Here the terrain opens up into moorland, and the (very clear) path winds gradually upwards, turning to the right side of the mountain before it starts to become quite steep. It is at this point you'll start to get some serious visual payoff for your exertions, with Suilven ahead of you and Cul Mor to the right, two more of the region's signature sharp-sided mountains.

The path continues on a steep ascent, turning to stone steps as you near the first summit ridge. You might need to stop for breath, but you will be propelled along by the constant promise of the rewards waiting for you at the top. And you will not be disappointed as you take your first steps onto the summit, where you'll find yourself within a sea of natural sandstone turrets. It feels almost otherworldly, with strange rock formations linked via narrow pathways and ridges, and almost anywhere you stand has panoramic 360-degree vistas. To the west you can glimpse the Summer Isles, to the north the Point of Stoer; Suilven to the northeast completes this impressive list of Scottish landscapes.

Once you arrive at this first summit, we recommend a proper break and tucking into the tea, snacks or whatever refreshment you have brought. After that, if you feel you have the legs and head for a bit more height, it's time to head to the Western Summit. This requires a few slightly tricky sections of scrambling and has some dangerous drops, so do consider your confidence and experience before tackling it. You'll need to take the weather into account too, as the winds up at the top of Stac Pollaidh can be vicious and indeed really quite dangerous. Please make sure that you are confident they will not hamper your progress on this last section.

After winding your way up mountainside paths, tackling steep steps and navigating some tricky scrambles, conquering the Western Summit gives you a real buzz. You'll certainly have earned your feeling of pure isolation as you take your seat on Scotland's ceiling. If you haven't already done so, now is the time to scoff a victory sandwich!

Tip: If you have time after climbing back down, head to nearby Loch Lurgainn for a cooling dip. (In the warmer months, at least!) It's bliss for sore post-hiking muscles, has its own little beach, and is conveniently located just behind the carpark. We took a cooler of beers and made some lunch on a little cooker – the perfect way to end the experience.

When it comes to extraordinary places to stay in the UK, you'll be hard pressed to find anywhere else quite like this. The Isle of Lewis' traditional crofting village, Gearrannan Blackhouses promises an adventure like no other. Sleeping in the original thatched, stone-walled dwellings, hidden away on a remote island immersed in history, you'll feel like you've been transported back to a simpler time, living in harmony with nature.

Time	multi-day
Fitness	low
Cost	affordable
Effort	medium
Equipment	none
Transport	car required

The Outer Hebrides, Scotland

Staying in Gearrannan Blackhouses

Is this for me?

The first thing you need to know about the village of Gearrannan is just how remote it is. It's like its own little enclave far away from the rest of the UK, situated on the far northwestern coast of the Isle of Lewis. As you can imagine, getting there from the mainland isn't exactly easy, with public transport links pretty tricky and hours of driving required. But if you feel like the journey is part of the adventure, then you'll love this trip. The Outer Hebrides are wild, untouched Scotland at its most stunning – and this adventure takes you to one of their remotest corners.

The adventure

To kick this adventure off, you will need to map out your journey from start to finish, as you're heading to one of the most remote, northerly parts of Scotland.

Ferries depart from Uig on the north coast of the Isle of Skye and Ullapool on the west coast of the mainland. From these locations you can catch a ferry to either Tarbert on Harris (the southern third of the island) or Stornoway on Lewis (the northern two-thirds of the island). If you take the Stornoway option, you will then have a 40-minute drive north to the village. If you're taking the longer drive from Tarbert, you'll have an amazing introduction to the scenery as you pass through boulder-strewn landscapes and wind between gorgeous lochs.

> **Tip:** Before you start driving north from Stornoway, stop off at the large Co-op in town. The cottages you'll be staying in are self-catered, and there's pretty much nowhere to get supplies beyond this point. If your ferry docks at Tarbert, either stock up in Skye before boarding or make a slight detour to go via Stornoway, which will take your drive to around the one hour 20 minute mark.

Nestled in a small cove, the remote village of Gearrannan boasts its own white-sand beach with jaw-dropping views of the Atlantic Ocean. But the real stars of the show here are the 10 or so traditional Hebridean cottages that make up the village. The cottages came to be known as 'Blackhouses' in contrast to the newer 'White Houses', which boasted designs that separated humans from their livestock – unlike the Blackhouses. Constructed in the late 1800s, these small thatch-roofed dwellings were once common across the islands. For centuries they were home to crofters – tenant farmers common in rural Scotland – who used them to shelter from the brutal winter conditions on this stretch of coast. The signature central chimneys were designed to keep the inhabitants warm.

For all their ingenious design and scenic location, the cottages were abandoned for a long time due to their need for regular upkeep. Thankfully, in the 1960s a local trust refurbished them and made them available for travellers to rent, breathing new life into the area and preserving these unique buildings for future generations.

One of the cottages is now a museum, chronicling the history of the community, which is well worth checking out. But to get a sense of just how remote the village is, you need to head out into nature. In both directions along the coast there are walking routes, which have sensational views not only of the ocean but also of the village, hunkered down in its little bay. As the cove is relatively sheltered from the elements, it's perfect for a swim or settling down on the cliffs to watch the sunset over the ocean.

Between the isolated location and the intriguing accommodation, you'll definitely want to stay here for at least a night. One of the Blackhouses has even been converted into a hostel, so you can definitely travel on a budget. Whichever option you go for, book in advance to avoid missing out.

If you hire a whole cottage, you'll find the insides are basic but have everything you need. Really, that's the charm of this experience. It's a rare opportunity to immerse yourself in history, to strip things back to their simplest elements: good company or blissful solitude in a wild and beautiful place.

Sailing the Inner Hebrides

If you are looking for an unforgettable way to experience the magic of the Inner Hebrides, a rugged archipelago in western Scotland, then there's no better option than taking to the water. This adventure will take you to the edge of the British Isles, offering you a completely unique perspective on the UK. Add in a classic sailboat, and you have all the ingredients for an unforgettable slow-travel experience.

Time full day

Fitness low

Cost costly

Effort medium

Equipment none

Transport best by car

Is this for me?

Ultimately this is just a day of sitting on a boat, so from a physical exertion perspective it certainly isn't the most challenging adventure. However, what it lacks in physicality it more than makes up for in the feeling of adventure you will experience as you glide through the water powered only by the elements.

Part of the Inner Hebrides' charm is their remoteness, but this does naturally mean they're a bit difficult to reach, especially via public transport.

The adventure

The Inner Hebrides is an archipelago off the west coast of mainland Scotland, famed for its jaw-dropping beauty. As with most islands, there aren't many better ways of exploring than by boat. There are plenty of group tours on offer, but by joining one you do run the risk of having a somewhat cookie-cutter experience. If you're looking for a more adventurous way to explore these magical waters, then there really is only one man for the job: Mark Jardine.

Mark lives on Iona and is the proud owner of Birthe Marie, a 1933 Danish sailboat. Over a number of years, he lovingly restored it to pristine condition and now, alongside his wife and sons, he runs small-group tours around the surrounding Hebridean islands.

The majority of excursions embark from the small port of Fionnphort on the far southwest coast of Mull, a 75-minute drive from Tobermory, and range in length from half- to full-day trips. If you are staying on Iona then you can also arrange for Mark to pick you up from there. The trips can take you anywhere in the area, depending on what you want to see and the conditions that day. This gives you access to some extraordinary corners of the Hebridean islands, of which there are around 80.

Stepping onto the boat, two things will strike you immediately. Firstly, the boat itself is absolutely gorgeous. With its faded pastel colours, hand-stitched seams, weathered wood and peeling paint, stepping aboard the Birthe Marie is like entering a Rauschenberg painting. Secondly, you'll notice Mark's air of calm. He's just the sort of guy who puts you at ease from the minute you meet him – softly spoken, welcoming and very laid-back.

For our trip, we wanted to prioritize seeing the local puffins. On Mark's advice we set sail for the Treshnish Islands, a small archipelago only two hours from Fionnphort with the wind in your sails. If you opt for this excursion you'll find the journey flies by as you glide through an array of ocean blues, absorbing Mark's local insight as you go. He is a fountain of knowledge, and has an infectious passion for his home islands.

Reaching Lunga, the Treshnish archipelago's largest island, you drop anchor and make your way to the rugged shoreline on a small inflatable rowing boat. Thousands of puffins, kittiwakes and guillemots fill the air overhead, making it feel like you're the only humans around on this bird-filled isle.

You only need a couple of hours to see the highlights on Lunga, long enough to eat lunch, wander the 81-hectare island, and of course admire its most famous inhabitants: the puffins. They are hard to miss, lining the cliff tops where they land with seemingly no fear of humans, meaning you can get within a metre of them. They are beautiful birds, and being able to observe them at such close quarters and in such a dramatic setting makes for a special experience.

Sailing silently back to the drop-off point on Mull gives you a moment to gaze out at the horizon and reflect on your day. It's easy to forget that we live on a set of wild islands, and to experience them like this is undoubtedly good for the soul. In Mark's own words, an adventure on Birthe Marie offers 'an unhurried drinking-in of the landscape. The boat fits into the coastal scene, disturbing little, quietly finding her way into places hidden from life at shore.'

If that image isn't enough to tempt you into this adventure, nothing will be!

Don't forget

Layers! As with all Scottish adventures, layers are key. Make sure you check the weather before you go and pack accordingly. We went from sunny to windswept, cold to positively hot over the course of the day, and so were constantly adding and removing garments. This may sound like an obvious pointer, but you really don't want to be stuck out on a boat at sea for a whole day and be cold!

Tip: You will not have access to a shop – or indeed fresh water – from the moment you leave land until your return, so you'll need to bring your meals with you. If you are leaving from Iona, remember that there is only one shop on the island, so you'll need to pick up supplies in good time. On Mull, there's a small Post Office shop in Fionnphort where you can get supplies for a relatively basic packed lunch. If you want something more sophisticated, you will need to get that from Tobermory, on the other side of the island.

Driving Scotland's Snow Roads

Winter in the UK can get a bad press, but try out an adventure which embraces its cold beauty and you might just find yourself rethinking your preconceptions. Scotland's Snow Roads take you on a scenic 90-mile (145-km) route along the UK's highest public road, with views of the wild Cairngorms National Park. Gazing out at the snow-capped mountains, you'll appreciate that this breathtaking scenery is at its most dramatic in the winter.

Time multi-day

Fitness low

Cost cheap

Effort medium

Equipment none

Transport car required

Is this for me?

This is essentially a road trip, and so is very accessible for people of all ages and abilities. You can stop as little or as often as you like, adjusting the experience to be more action-packed or more relaxed. If you like putting on your favourite playlist and cruising through epic nature, then you are most likely going to enjoy this one.

This adventure offers a pretty pure hit of Scotland at its winter best. That said, even out of the coldest months, the mountains will most likely still sport a sprinkling of snow, and so those views will deliver!

The adventure

The Snow Roads is a scenic driving route located in Cairngorms National Park, an area of 1748 square miles (4527 square km) in the northeast of Scotland. It stretches from the market town of Blairgowrie in the south to the Highland town of Grantown-on-Spey.

We tackled it over the course of two days, but you could do a section in an afternoon or indeed spread it out over the course of a week – it just depends on your time and appetite. This route is quite popular, so it's wise to book accommodation in advance if you do go for the multi-day option. And as with any car journey, make sure you've got a good few playlists sorted and are stocked up on snacks!

Part of our road trip philosophy is to go with the flow, to stop when you want rather than at rigidly pre-decided points. If you ask us, the spontaneity is half of the fun of a road trip! That said, to make the most of your time it's probably wise to note down a few choice places to stop along the route which fit your plans. Still, it's really all about the drive, and simply soaking in this incredible section of mountainous Scotland.

Activities

Enjoying the Snow Roads is, as the saying goes, all about the journey rather than the destination. There are so many places worth exploring along this action-packed route – here are just a few which we enjoyed, starting from the northern end of the route and working down

Kayaking/Rafting on the River Spey

If you are looking for an adventurous first stop, one which will enable you to see the surrounding landscapes from an entirely different perspective than through your car windows, then why not take to the waters of the River Spey? Those after an adrenaline hit should think about rafting the section between Ballindalloch and Knockando, which has grade-II rapids including a steep section called the Washing Machine.

You don't need to be an expert, however, as there are companies in Aviemore who can take you out for the day – children aged six and over can join, so it's a great one if you're travelling with family. Further downstream the river calms a bit, and you can canoe, kayak or even paddle board. Do still take care though – the Spey is one of the fastest-flowing rivers in the UK, so it isn't for the faint-hearted, especially at times of high rainfall. We'd suggest you go with a guide unless you're fairly experienced.

Blairfindy Moor Dark Sky Discovery Site

Eleven minutes' drive south of Ballindalloch, just southwest of the Glenlivet Distillery, is the second International Dark Sky Park in Scotland – and the most northerly in the world! Stop here to see some of the best night-sky views in the UK, with exceptional stargazing in clear weather. There are dark-sky tours available locally, which can give you professional insight into what you're seeing, but it's also a great place for some casual stargazing. Winter is when the skies tend to be at their darkest and clearest, making this a great cold-weather stop.

Braemar

Just an hour's drive south, sitting at the eastern gateway to the Cairngorms, Braemar is a charming little village surrounded by some of the area's highest mountains. Here you'll find several good places to eat, an abundance of dramatic hiking routes leading into the peaks, and the famous Braemar Castle. If you want to add a splash of luxury to your trip, book a stay at the Fife Arms. This beautifully designed nineteenth-century hunting lodge combines traditional extravagance with modern flair to create an incredible slice of Scottish luxury.

The Linn of Dee

Located just outside Braemar, this beautiful piece of geology is where the mighty River Dee squeezes through a narrow gap in the rock, creating a unique natural sculpture. It is a great place to stop for a quick picnic (as Queen Victoria liked to do) or hike the scenic trails that surround it.

The above suggestions just scratch the surface on what you can do here. Hiking, watersports, historical ruins, rare species of birds and wildlife, distilleries, lochs, waterfalls… It's hard not to find something you might like along the route. And of course, you can always just kick back and relax in the comfort of your car, watching the dramatic scenery roll past.

Don't forget

While taking it slow is highly recommended (especially in the winter months), do be courteous to other drivers and let them overtake on the small lanes. Locals still need to go about their daily lives, after all.

Wild adventure in Assynt

If you want wild Scotland, this is the place for you. Covering a northwestern swathe of the Scottish Highlands, Assynt is teeming with extraordinary mountains, ancient castles and immense lochs. Pristine white beaches soften the craggy shoreline, and the NC500 route links up some of the most spectacular sights. Assynt just encapsulates that awe-inspiring feeling that runs through the veins of Scotland.

Time multi-day

Fitness low

Cost affordable

Effort medium

Equipment none

Transport car required

Is this for me?

The scenic, 516-mile (847-km) North Coast 500 (NC500) runs through the heart of Assynt. If you are embarking on this epic route, you should give it the time it truly deserves, so this isn't an adventure to squeeze into a day. Factor in a jam-packed schedule full of incredible places to explore.

This adventure will require a car or a campervan to cover the large distances. Once you're on the road (see page 139), it's really up to you where you head. With the right to roam and to wild camp in a tent wherever, this adventure is one to make your own. This flexibility and the option to change plans on a whim makes it perfect for families – kids and rigid plans are rarely a good mix! Note that the rules for wild camping are different for campervans, so be sure to check them ahead of time if relevant.

The adventure

The Assynt region, just north of Ullapool, is one of the harder-to-reach corners of the UK. Once you're there, though, you'll find many of the most impressive sights are well connected by the world-famous NC500 route, making it quite straightforward to explore if you're driving.

This adventure requires you to prepare as you would for all Scottish adventures. Lots of layers, bug spray, a thermos and of course a camera to capture all those dramatic landscapes. You're really spoiled for choice in terms of outdoor adventures here, so you can adapt your itinerary to suit your interests. For us, four places in particular stood out; all but one are just a short detour from the NC500.

Kylesku Bridge

Kylesku is famous for having one of the most beautiful bridges in the UK, if not the world, with its distinct, pared-back design. It curves gently over Loch a' Chàirn Bhàin, giving you views over the water without distracting too much from the loch's stunning natural beauty. Driving over the bridge is an experience in itself, but be sure to pull over in the carpark on the south side of the bridge and take the short walk to a viewpoint afterwards so you can absorb the unique design.

Wailing Widow Falls

Your next stop is just a few minutes south of the bridge. When we first saw Allt Chranaidh, also called the Wailing Widows Falls, we were stopped dead in our tracks. It's one of those views that has you doing a double take, to make sure it's actually real. The falls are the result of water from the windswept mountaintop Loch Gainmhich flowing right off a sheer cliff face, plummeting 30 metres into the valley below.

The scale of the scenery immediately makes you feel tiny. This waterfall is vast and powerful, and acts as a humbling reminder of how small we really are in the face of nature. You are able to view the waterfall from both the top and the bottom. The view from below is still quite magnificent, and you can walk along the river bed to get to the plunge pool at the bottom of the cascading water. If you're able, we highly recommend the short walk to the top of the waterfall. Up here we found watching the show to be completely captivating.

Clachtoll Beach

Clachtoll is an absolute gem of a beach. Situated on the Bay of Clachtoll, 35 minutes' drive southwest of the Wailing Widow Falls, it's a popular stop along the NC500. But just follow the coast eastward, and you'll find some unreal, secluded sea-swimming spots without too many visitors. It's also a convenient overnight stop, as there's a great campground right by the beach. Given how spectacular it is, we wouldn't blame you for wanting to extend your time here!

Stac Pollaidh

Once you've had your fill of the beach, drive south along the coast for about an hour before heading inland slightly to Stac Pollaidh, an absolute must-visit if you're in the area. The hike up the mountain (see page 106) is short but steep; within an hour you will find yourself standing amid the giant rock stacks on the summit. Enjoy the view back down, surrounded by the Highlands in all their glory. This is, in our opinion, one of the best mountains in the whole of the UK.

We've only outlined a handful of the adventurous options available to you in Assynt. Our advice is to do your homework ahead of time so you know when to venture off the main NC500 route, and make sure you leave enough time to fit everything in! Of course, you can tackle it in any order, too. Ullapool makes a handy base if you'd like to visit these spots, with Stac Pollaidh only half an hour's drive away, and Kylesku Bridge under an hour.

Don't forget

Be mindful on the roads, and pull over to let people pass if you want to take your time about exploring. People live here, too, and navigating the roads can be very tricky alongside unfamiliar drivers. Don't be that tourist blocking the roads in peak travel season – it's OK to take it at a leisurely pace, but be respectful.

There is something about staying in a treehouse that will forever fill us with a sense of childlike excitement. Stepping outside the norm and climbing up into the canopy to spend the night creates a really pure version of that adventurous feeling. And the Treehouses at Lanrick combine that base of nostalgic excitement with a few more adult-friendly selling points – beauty, eco-friendly design, home comforts – to create a brilliant all-round experience.

Time	multi-day
Fitness	low
Cost	costly
Effort	low
Equipment	none
Transport	best by car

Loch Lomond & the Trossachs, Scotland

A night in Trossachs Treehouses

126

Is this for me?

This is a really easy-to-achieve adventure. One of the treehouses is wheelchair accessible, and for the rest, the easy climb up to them is the most physically demanding thing you'll need to do. Other than that, you can simply sit out on the deck of your treehouse sipping red wine and listening to the birds. If you are after adrenaline-fuelled fun then this won't quite meet your requirements, but if it's slow adventure you desire then the treehouses are hard to beat. The perfect getaway for couples wanting a relaxing break in nature, a stay at the Treehouses at Lanrick is also a great option if you have a child, as the cabins are spacious with lots of room for your little one to crawl or toddle around.

The adventure

The houses are built into the trees on the banks of the River Teith, just an hour's drive from both Edinburgh and Glasgow, making them very easy to get to. As you pull off the main road into the grounds of the estate in which they are situated you will quickly find yourself surrounded by nature. Follow the winding road until you reach your final off-grid destination.

The first thing that hits you is just how beautifully designed the treehouses are. Crafted from gorgeous old wood, they are wrapped around the trees in extremely pleasing geometric designs. Any stress you may have kicking about your system from the journey will soon fade away as you walk up the wooden steps to your cabin and onto your luxuriously large forest-viewing deck.

All the cabins have similar layouts and finishes. They are all made of reclaimed wood with modern touches, and the attention paid to the guest experience really makes them stand out. We stayed in Flycatcher and were greeted with a bottle of wine and a welcome hamper of fresh local produce, ready for our dinner in the fully equipped kitchen or out on the deck, where there's a large Weber barbecue. After eating, we poured a glass of wine and watched the stars come out, before cosying up by the fire (ready to go when you arrive) in the comfortable living room.

The whole space is designed to immerse you in nature without sacrificing your comfort. As well as enjoying a meal outdoors, you can even bathe there – you'll find a luxurious roll-top bath in a private area of decking, a spectacular little space where you can watch the branches swaying above you as you soak. And if it's too chilly to relax outside, you can still take in perfectly framed views of the surrounding woods through the living room windows, which allow light to flood in at varying angles throughout the day.

Needless to say, you'll have a memorable time just lounging around in your treehouse. But if you do manage to peel yourself off the sofa, you'll find several activities worth checking out in the grounds, as well as in the surrounding area. The River Teith is the lifeblood of the area, and it flows just a stone's throw from the treehouses, so we do recommend a leisurely riverside stroll to start your day. There are also two small huts built on the banks, complete with fire pits, which guests can use for picnics.

To get to know the river a little better, why not try your hand at fly-fishing for salmon or trout? The season runs from February to October, and the activity is free of charge, though you'll need to book in advance.

If you'd like to explore a little further afield, head to Loch Lomond and the Trossachs National Park. The whole area is an outdoor activities heaven, with hill walking, mountain climbing, bike trails, wild swimming and boat trips on the lochs.

A stay at the Treehouses at Lanrick is sure to rejuvenate you. The feeling of relaxation that comes from spending time in such close proximity to nature is energizing and will leave you with a big smile on your face. This is a slow and extremely comfortable adventure. We booked our stay here through Kip Hideaways.

Don't forget

This is Scotland, so the weather is predictably unpredictable. You should definitely take layers, but wellies are also handy in the wetter months so you can walk all the trails without getting soggy socks!

Winter on the edge of Britain

Explore beautifully desolate beaches, vast sand dunes and ancient sea caves, while you battle with every imaginable weather condition. Visiting the far north of the Scottish Highlands in the depths of winter provides a feeling of isolation you rarely get to experience in the modern world. It's a feeling that will stay with you a long while.

Time multi-day

Fitness medium

Cost affordable

Effort medium

Equipment none

Transport best by car

Is this for me?

Heading to this northern extremity in the middle of winter is not for everyone. If you balk at the thought of long journeys, turbulent weather and short hours of daylight, you should definitely sit this one out.

But for some of you, that description will have piqued your curiosity. If that's you, let us be the first to say that this off-season trip has its perks. Right at the top of Scotland, this wild, rugged and unpredictable coastline is ripe for adventure. It boasts sensational beaches, lochs and snow-capped mountains – and, most notably, a distinct lack of humans. This all combines to give you that off-grid feeling without having to travel to a far-off land.

This adventure has pretty poor transport links, so to really get stuck in and make the most of the incredible variety up here, a car is your best bet. Additionally, some of the activities we recommend require a fairly good level of mobility. If that's an issue for you, though, you can easily skip those and still have a spectacular experience.

The adventure

While this isn't some far-flung spot halfway round the world, it's still pretty remote. Inverness is the northernmost city in the UK, and the tiny village of Durness – a great base for this adventure – is almost three hours' drive further north than that. The sheer scale of this trip can feel daunting, but you'll enjoy breathtaking scenery along the entire way, making it feel like the adventure has started long before you arrive.

Preparation is as much about expectation as it is what to pack. Know that this adventure is all about getting stuck in and embracing the elements. You need to make sure you have got lots of layers and waterproofs.

The coast surrounding the small village of Durness is wild Scotland at its best. In the winter you may not see another soul for days, making it the perfect trip if you're after some solitude. That said, you'll find that the locals of Sutherland, the region around Durness, are extremely friendly if you run into them at any point!

As it takes quite a lot of effort to get here, we recommend finding somewhere cosy to hole up for a few days while you explore. We opted for Croft 103, hidden away on the coast 20 minutes' drive east of Durness. This eco-hideout is nestled in nature, overlooking Loch Eriboll, and about as secluded as it gets.

To put it simply, Croft 103 is one of the most beautifully designed places we have ever been lucky enough to stay. The sturdy stone walls and gently curved, low-slung roof hardly disrupt the natural landscape. The building's huge glass frontage frames the unmistakable peak of nearby Ben Hope and offers glorious views over the sea loch, inviting the wild landscapes inside. Every detail, material and feature of the interior is meticulously thought out. It's important to note that Croft 103 is a little more expensive than most places and most certainly not an integral part of this adventure, so if it doesn't work for your budget, simply look at other options in the area.

Despite the cosy comforts of the croft, we recommend you get up early(ish) to catch the sunrise from Balnakeil Beach. It's only five minutes' drive from Durness, and has a carpark from which it's an easy walk down to the beach.

The sweeping white sands of spectacular Balnakeil, framed by large dramatic dunes, make for a great beach walk. And if you're lucky, you won't be the only ones out for a stroll – the locals, a herd of cows, may be meandering along the shoreline in search of fresh water.

As well as the thin ribbon of beach, you'll want to explore the dunes. From up on the highest ones you'll be able to see for miles. In one direction, you can see snow-capped mountains. In the other, waves from the North Sea crash aggressively against huge rocks. And here is arguably the most spectacular view: the windswept coastline and icy blue sea, stretching away to the horizon.

If it's a particularly rainy day, Smoo Cave might be more appealing than the exposed sands of Balnakeil Beach. Set into limestone cliffs off Durness, the cave is accessible via a set of stairs cut into the rock. Its 15-metre-wide entrance is the largest of any sea cave in the UK. The inside of the cave is floodlit, illuminating a second chamber, where you can see a powerful 20-metre waterfall. It is pretty spectacular.

Finally, if you are looking to sample one of the most beautiful beaches in the area, make for Sango Bay. Under five minutes' drive from Smoo Cave, what it lacks in size it more than makes up for with golden sands and strange rock formations on which the waves crash. The nearby campsite, Sango Sands Oasis, is in a brilliant location – but camping here in the winter months isn't for the faint-hearted!

This adventure is one of the more extreme in the book, its weather and geography combining to bring you closer to nature and the elements. We found it to be a transformative adventure that made us view Scotland through a new lens.

Don't forget

Days are very short here in winter, so your window for exploring is quite short. Hit the road before the sun comes up each morning so you're out and about for sunrise. After it sets, nothing is cosier than holing up in your cabin, getting a fire going and relaxing.

Shops are few and far between, so the rule is if you need food and see a shop, you should stop. The same is true of petrol stations. That's just part and parcel of being so secluded.

The Green Loch & Ryvoan Bothy Trek

This memorable hike is located in Scotland's Cairngorms National Park, in the eastern Highlands. The route takes you around a perfect loop through ancient Scottish forests, past an emerald-green lake, to a bothy and up and down a mountain. It is fair to say that at no point will you find tackling it boring.

Time few hours

Fitness medium

Cost free

Effort medium

Equipment some recommended

Transport best by car

Is this for me?

As Scottish hikes go this is one of the easier ones, coming in at just under six miles and with fairly flat terrain for much of the route. There is only one section of ascent that will test your lungs a bit, and of course its accompanying descent. It can also get quite slippery underfoot, especially in the winter. If you're a little shaky with heights or don't think you've got the fitness to climb a steep section, then this might not be the adventure for you.

On the other hand, if you are looking for a half-day deep dive into the breathtaking beauty of the Cairngorms National Park, don't miss this! This hike has a little bit of everything, and is an ideal adventure for keen walkers.

The adventure

This hike begins just 15 minutes' drive from the town of Aviemore, at the Glenmore Visitor Centre. You can park your car here, and it's also where the fairly regular bus from Aviemore stops. The walk starts off nice and gently, following the well-marked path next to the visitor centre. You'll then pass the Cairngorm Reindeer Centre (which offers hill trips to see Britain's only free-ranging herd of reindeer), after which a trail of blue markers points you through the Caledonian pines.

After only half an hour or so of weaving in between trees and climbing over their thick, protruding roots, you'll hit the hike's first milestone: Lochan Uaine. Also known as the Green Loch, this small lake is famous for its deep emerald waters. Its mesmerizing colours make it an ideal place to pause. You could even go for a quick dip should it take your fancy, but beware – like most places in Scotland, it will be cold!

After you've admired the loch and caught your breath, rejoin the path and follow it until it forks left towards Nethy Bridge. Soon after that, you'll see a simple stone building called Ryvoan Bothy. This bothy has stone benches for sleeping on and a little fireplace. It's perfect for a tea and snack stop before setting off on the most challenging leg of the journey.

Follow the pathway ahead and to the left of the bothy door, leading you up the incline to Meall a' Bhuachaille. This path is steep, but with every step you take you gain increasingly more spectacular views. You'll find a great vantage point to take in Abernethy Forest, which is the largest expanse of native forest in the UK.

The summit is incredibly exposed, and you will more often than not find yourselves at the mercy of the Scottish elements. Luckily there is a cairn which acts as a pretty effective windbreaker. This shelter makes a great spot for a quick sandwich, depending on your timings.

When it's time to descend, follow the winding track down the other side of Meall a' Bhuachaille – a much more gentle slope than the one that you took on the way up. The track leads to a brand new terrain; as the ground begins to level out you'll see beautiful, bizarrely shaped trees, sculpted by the wind. Now somewhat protected from the wind by the mountainside behind you, you'll find it even easier to appreciate the beautiful landscape on this last section of the hike. You'll thoroughly enjoy weaving through the forest section back towards the visitor centre.

Don't forget

This trek has plenty of spectacular spots to break for food and drink, so make sure you're prepared on that front.

Also, make sure you're aware of and adhere to the Bothy Code. Respect the bothy by leaving no trace, both inside and outside the shelter. You can find more on this on page 223.

Wild camping on the Isle of Mull

It's hard to beat the feeling of wild camping. There's just something about pitching a tent wherever you fancy and spending the night under the stars that is incredibly freeing. If you're looking for this experience, there can't be many places better to try it than the beautiful coast of Mull.

Time	multi-day
Fitness	medium
Cost	free
Effort	medium
Equipment	required
Transport	best by car

Is this for me?

Wild camping strips life back to its basics, embedding you in nature and allowing you to focus on one thing at a time. In some ways you could say it is the perfect remedy to the hectic pace of modern life. If you try it, you'll find there aren't many more beautiful places to wake up than on a Scottish island.

What's more, due to Scotland's 2003 Land Reform Act, you have the right to roam and camp on most unenclosed land. This means you can easily extend the adventure and check out a few different spots if you find one night isn't enough, without scrabbling to book last-minute accommodation.

This adventure does require a good degree of mobility. If that doesn't work for you, then luckily you'll find there are plenty of other ways to enjoy the beauty of Mull (see pages 114 and 163). Tobermory, the main town on Mull, is one of Scotland's prettiest ports, lined with colourful housing; it's the perfect place to spend an afternoon. Simply driving the perimeter of the island is another great activity, offering some breathtaking scenery and giving you complete flexibility on how much you stop and explore on foot.

The adventure

You know what they say – fail to prepare, prepare to fail. We might not put it in quite such extreme terms, but this experience is definitely improved if you plan ahead. That prep should begin by packing your kit a couple of days before you leave home. Make sure you've got all the things you need for a night under the stars, like your tent, sleeping bags, mats, torches and stove. This may seem simple, but with the million things you've got to organize, forgetting the head torches or teabags is easily done. You'll kick yourself once you're out in the wild, believe us!

The second largest of the Inner Hebridean islands, Mull is a west-coast gem. With over 300 miles (483 km) of coastline it boasts some of the most extraordinary white-sand beaches in the UK.

Its relatively remote location means visitors need to get a boat from the mainland – ferries from Oban, Lochaline and Kilchoan all take under an hour. Due to the journey, Mull has relatively few tourists, especially on its southwest coast, where we recommend you head.

This stretch of coast is wild, rugged and quiet, making it an incredible place to set up camp. You don't need to have an exact place in mind before you set off – just keep your eyes peeled for promising spots. That said, it's a good idea to have a flexible plan and a rough idea of where you might like to stop before you set off, just so you don't end up stuck somewhere unsuitable.

> **Tip: When choosing where to pitch up for the night, we recommend you use Google Earth to get your bearings. It allows you to see the type of terrain you will be dealing with in a bit more detail, and we find it helpful in deciphering the exact characteristics of the coastline. You'll also want to check the tide times and the weather forecast.**

From Tobermory, Mull's biggest town, drive for an hour and a half southwest towards the small village of Fionnphort, from where the ferries to Iona leave (see page 114). Fionnphort is the last and in fact only place in the immediate area where you can buy food and supplies. You can find some basics at the little Post Office.

Once stocked up, take the only road south out of town. This single-track lane will lead you in the direction of a small place called Fidden. From here onwards, the coastline has plenty of gorgeous sandy beaches, hidden coves and rugged rock formations. Part of the fun of this adventure is picking your own spot to make camp, so find one that is somewhat sheltered from the elements. Once satisfied, set up your tent and if required find firewood.

Once you're set up, you are free to explore. Swim in the crystal-clear waters. Discover sea thrift-covered tidal islands. When the sun starts to set, start your campfire, or prime your stove, and cook a warming dinner. This far coast of Mull is remote, wild and beautifully peaceful.

You may not be entirely alone though... If you're lucky you might witness the herd of swimming cows! They're known to take a sunset dip on the beaches of this part of Mull. The story goes that a local farmer once took them to one of the nearby tidal islands to graze. Apparently the experience has entered their collective memory, as they still visit the shallows. We were lucky enough to see this, and it was one of the most extraordinary quirks of nature we've ever witnessed.

This adventure really captures the unique magic of camping wild. You'll feel immersed in nature for the entirety of the experience. That's especially thanks to the lack of a phone signal or any distractions. You'll really get the chance to slow down and absorb the beauty that surrounds you. You will not be forgetting your night spent under the stars on this remote Scottish coast in a hurry.

Don't forget

You need to ensure your own safety when you adventure this far into the wild. Remember: there is little to no help available to you. You will also need to take care of the environment, so follow the Scottish Outdoor Access Code. Here are some important notes from the code:

- Ideally, use a stove rather than starting a fire. If you do start a fire, though, ensure it's small and under control. You should never light one after a dry spell or in woodlands, farmland or near buildings. Please ensure you put it out properly and leave no trace.

- When going to the toilet, make sure you choose a spot at least 30 metres from open water sources such as rivers, lakes and streams. If you do a number two you need to dig a small hole and bury it – as far away from water sources, buildings and farm animals as possible.

- Remove all traces of your tent pitch and take all litter, including food waste, with you when you leave.

A winter trek on the Cairngorm Plateau

Of all the extremities here in the UK, the Cairngorm National Park has to be one of the most spectacular. Its wild, mountainous expanses are a must for those wanting to see Scotland at its most dramatic. The national park sees the most snowfall in the UK, with its habitat being classed as ecologically arctic; unsurprisingly, it's the perfect place for an epic winter hike. The walk across the exposed, frozen plateau is one of the most unique routes we have on these shores.

Time few hours

Fitness medium

Cost free

Effort high

Equipment none

Transport public transport available

Is this for me?

This adventure requires a decent level of fitness, organization and a bit of nerve. The area is infamous for the 1970s Cairngorm Plateau disaster, in which several school students and a teacher died after getting lost there. This tragedy serves as a warning to make sure you are thorough with your planning. It is really important to have a clear understanding of the weather and to suitably prepare for it. If you do so, then you'll find this adventure is actually quite straightforward – it's a very well-trodden route, and extremely popular with hikers due to its incredible scenery.

The adventure

First things first: make sure you are properly prepared for this adventure. The weather in the mountains can be brutal and changeable, so make sure you have a really accurate understanding of what the weather is predicted to do that day. Prep also includes making sure you are very clear on directions, as phone signal up there is basically non-existent, and of course ensuring you've got the right gear (page 222).

Tip: There are a fair few hiking shops in the nearby town of Aviemore, so talk to the staff there to get their take on current conditions. It's also worth checking with the Cairngorm Mountain ski resort.

There are several routes across the plateau; we took the shortest and in turn most achievable, which starts at the Cairngorm ski centre.

To get to the ski centre, you can either drive up and park in the large carpark or take the 31 bus from Aviemore. The centre is at an altitude of 590 metres, and once you're there you are neatly positioned to get to the plateau without too much hiking. From the centre you follow the tracks up until you reach the top of the ski route – depending on conditions and how fast you want to go, this usually takes an hour or so. The gradient is quite intense at points, and of course it's harder going in the snow.

Once at the top of the ski route, take the deep stone steps right to the top of the plateau, where you will see a summit cairn and a trig point. Should the visibility allow it, you will have some of the most dramatic views in the whole of the UK from up here. Take as long as you'd like to savour your achievement, gazing out over the UK's second-highest mountain, Ben Macdui, and the towering summits of Cairn Lochan and Stob Coire.

From this point you have several options of further routes up, many winding over the surrounding mountains and ridges. We chose to set up camp for an hour instead, using a trig point as shelter from the wind, and sat back with a thermos of tea to watch the sunset turn the clouds from oranges and pinks into deep reds. If you choose this option make sure you get your timings right, both in terms of getting up there close to sunset and getting back down. You must allow yourself enough light, so set off soon after the sun has set to make it down before it's completely dark. It's worth taking a head torch as a backup, but don't rely on this as it's easy to get disoriented in the dark.

Once you judge it's time to leave, you can simply retrace your steps back down to the ski centre. You can't help but feel small when you're hiking across such a vast, arctic-like wilderness, which makes the trek a pretty humbling experience.

Don't forget

If you're heading up in winter, consider bringing crampons. They do make life easier in very snowy conditions.

A road trip across Lewis and Harris

You will struggle to find a purer hit of adventure than this excursion. Exploring the Outer Hebridean isle of Lewis and Harris is like nothing else. Right on the edge of the UK, this Scottish gem surely deserves a spot among the most beautiful islands in the world.

Time multi-day

Fitness medium

Cost affordable

Effort medium

Equipment some recommended

Transport car required

Is this for me?

With this Hebridean island, you're in for a long haul. It's a considerable distance from most of the UK, so you have to commit to the journey, which includes a lot of driving and then a car ferry from either Uig on Skye or Ullapool on the mainland. Also, the weather is incredibly variable. So if you like your island retreats dry and sunny, this adventure isn't for you. But if you are keen to experience some of the UK's most remote, rugged and wild beauty, then we would highly recommend you tackle this one!

As with all road trips, this requires a car. When it comes to fitness levels, you can pick and choose your stops and activities accordingly.

The adventure

Getting here is tricky, especially if you are planning to drive up from the Borders, England or Wales. If you have time, though, you can turn that to your advantage by adding more mini-adventures on your way up! The obvious stop is the Isle of Skye, which is easily accessible by car as there is a bridge connecting it to the mainland. The island is jam-packed with places to check out, but our favourites are in its northern reaches. Not only is this area much less visited than the rest of Skye, it's also where the ferry departs from, making it convenient for exploring on a pitstop.

This adventure is a road trip, so it couldn't be easier to prepare for. Make sure you bring your favourite snacks for the road, and put together a good playlist or two. Pack plenty of layers, and chuck some camping equipment in the boot if you have space. Really, there's no one-size-fits-all approach here – just pack what you need for the kind of adventure you want to have.

You'll have a plethora of options once you're on the islands, with over 840 square miles (2176 square km) of exceptional beauty to explore.

Lewis and Harris is, somewhat counterintuitively, one island. The two halves are often referred to separately, with Lewis comprising the top half and Harris the bottom. The island has a network of roads, which makes it perfect for exploration, and some very dramatic landscapes. During the seven days we were there, not once did we get bored of looking out of the window.

We only touched the surface in our week-long road trip, but here are a handful of our favourite things to do and see.

The Golden Road

A 21-mile (34-km) single-track loop road, it winds around lochs, derelict huts and bizarre rock formations in the west of the Isle of Harris.

Surfing

The Isle of Lewis and Harris has a spectacular coastline, so make the most of it! The island's exposure to the Atlantic makes it a prime spot to catch a wave. Check out Scarista, Luskentyre, Seilebost and Traigh Mhòr Beach. If you aren't able to bring a board with you, check out Surf Lewis and Harris in Sandwick near Stornoway, the island's capital; they can provide board rental and general information about watersports on the island.

Sea swimming

Scarista is also a great spot for a sea swim. This long stretch of white sand on the southwest coast of Harris is bordered by extraordinarily turquoise water. If you can pluck up the courage for a cold plunge, you'll find yourself invigorated as you soak up the views of the surrounding Hebridean mountains. Be safe though – the currents can be dangerous and unpredictable, so check before going in.

Fresh seafood

The waters surrounding the island are brimming with all kinds of sea life, many of which find their way onto local menus. If you're staying in to cook your own seafood feast, ask the locals for advice to find out where and when the fishing boats come in. People are extremely generous here, so be ready for a bounty. We ended up with bags of delicious, ultra-fresh seafood.

Camping

Lewis and Harris is the perfect place for this style of travel, so whether it's with a roof tent, ground tent or campervan, we highly recommend taking this stripped-back, closer to nature approach to your adventure for at least a night or two. We find you can really take in the natural, raw beauty of the island when you live amid it like this. Wild camping is allowed with tents, and there are many spots in beautiful locations available for campervans offering unrivalled proximity to some of the UK's most priceless views. It is important not to park in undesignated areas or to block up the passing places along the small lanes.

St Kilda

If you have time to extend your stay in the region, add on a day trip to St Kilda from Harris. This isolated archipelago around 55 miles (89 km) to the west of Harris almost feels lost to time. The village here was abandoned in 1930 after nearly 4000 years of the island being permanently inhabited, and the village remains still stand relatively intact today. With the highest sea cliffs in Britain, St Kilda is the most important sea-bird breeding station in this part of Europe, with guillemots, fulmars and puffins all nesting here. Boat trips to St Kilda only run between April and September, up to six times per week. You can book from a couple of different companies, both of which depart from Leverburgh Harbour in South Harris. You've got to plan ahead here.

Don't forget

Lewis and Harris is a remote island – make sure to plan ahead for fuel and supplies so that you don't end up having to cut the adventure short.

Discovering Tyninghame Beach

The term 'Hidden Gem' is bandied about a bit too much, but in the case of Tyninghame Beach, it is perhaps appropriate. A vast stretch of uninterrupted sand on Scotland's southeastern coast, the beach is accessible via a series of intricate forest pathways, miraculously only half an hour's drive from Edinburgh. Home to the famous Bass Rock and a set of dunes, Tyninghame is the perfect spot for a long walk and cold-water dip.

Time few hours

Fitness low

Cost free

Effort medium

Equipment none

Transport car required

Is this for me?

This adventure really surprised us. We were (perhaps naively) completely unaware of the beauty this stretch of the Scottish coast holds, and so the process of discovering it was eye-opening. If you're wanting to veer off the beaten track of Scottish adventure then it's a great option. What's more, with it being only a 30-minute drive from the capital, it makes for a short, cheap and easy-to-achieve adventure. That said, realistically you will need a car for this one, unless you're staying close enough that cycling is an option, as there are no public transport links.

The adventure

If you're driving here, simply put Limetree Walk, East Lothian into your navigation app and make your way to the very end of the track, where you will find a carpark. This is where you leave the last traces of civilization behind and make your way towards the wild, windswept beach. To get there, simply follow the signs, passing through woods and trails lined by sea buckthorn hedges on your way. After 15 minutes or so you will land on the sand of Tyninghame.

The scale of the place is the first thing that will strike you, with an enormous expanse of sand running up the coast and leading your eye to the mighty Bass Rock, a dramatic island situated just over a mile offshore. Visit when the tide is low and, to your right, you'll see a big network of pools home to an array of sea life.

The sand is flat and golden, making it perfect for sunbathing, running and games, and walking along it takes around 40 minutes at a gentle pace. This adventure is really all about slowing down and absorbing the Scottish elements, taking your time to meander between the rock pools and sheltering from the wind in the long grass of the dunes. Tyninghame is a great natural 'refresh' button that is pressed simply by being there.

Activities

Tyninghame Beach is really well positioned to explore some of the other treasures of this East Lothian coastline. If you'd like to extend your time here, we'd suggest:

Bass Rock Tours

Setting off from the Scottish Seabird Centre, which is positioned at the far north end of the beach and has a carpark of its own, these boat tours take you to the largest northern gannet colony in the world at Bass Rock. Ranging from an hour-long catamaran cruise around the island to the 'Three Island Seabird Safari' which includes exploring Bass Rock on foot, the tours have something for everyone.

Seacliff Beach

Another beauty of a beach, and ideal if you like the thrill of discovering the lesser-known local spots. Seacliff is a short drive up the coast from Tyninghame, and boasts dramatic views of the clifftop ruins of Tantallon Castle.

Drift Café

A short drive north from the Tyninghame carpark, just beyond the Scottish Seabird Centre, Drift consists of old shipping containers perched on the cliffs with excellent views of the Firth of Forth. But for us the real star of the show is the food, which ranges from delicious homemade cakes and treats to beautifully prepared locally caught seafood slap-ups. Whether you eat in or take away, this place is a winner.

Sit back and enjoy as the setting sun illuminates the iconic Neist Point lighthouse. Watch it turn the lighthouse and cliffs on the far west coast of Skye varying shades of pink, in a spectacular show put on by Mother Nature at one of the UK's geographical extremities. It's wonderful to witness it with your own eyes.

Time	few hours
Fitness	low
Cost	free
Effort	low
Equipment	none
Transport	car required

The Inner Hebrides, Scotland

Sunset at Neist Point

Is this for me?

If you are a fan of sunsets and dramatic Scottish landscapes, then you are going to like this adventure. Other than the journey to get there, everything about this experience is easily doable. It's also accessible to most people; you can park very close to the nearest viewpoint and so only a small amount of walking is necessary.

The adventure

Neist Point is a peninsula that reaches out into the ocean on the west coast of Skye. It is one of the island's most-photographed landmarks, due to the perfect positioning of the lighthouse, which was built here in 1909.

It's also one of the hardest places to get to on the island, taking a little over an hour to drive from Portree due to many of the roads being small and single-track. The journey itself is gorgeous, taking you from the east to northwest coasts of Skye and introducing you to the island's exposed, rugged landscapes along the way. We'd suggest heading to the west of the island well before sunset if possible, so you can visit some of the other beautiful spots in the area. We took a short walk to Varkasaig Beach when we visited, and Dunvegan Castle and Gardens is another place worth exploring.

As the day draws to a close, make your way to Neist Point for the spectacular sunset show. We took some snacks and drinks with us, and a couple of camping chairs. If you'd also like to bring some food, don't make the mistake of trying to grab supplies nearby; you'll need to stop at one of the bigger towns, like Portree.

This is a cool adventure at any time of day, but due to its westerly location the ideal time to visit is around sunset. Check what time the sun is due to set while you're visiting, and work back from there to make sure you arrive at the perfect time.

If you follow your navigation app to Neist Point, the road will eventually come to an end; this is where the carpark is. At peak times it can get very busy, though, so you may need to find a spot along the side of the road before you get to the official carpark instead. From here, veer right along the clifftop and walk for five to 10 minutes to the first viewpoint. You'll be able to see the whole of the point, with the lighthouse neatly positioned at its end. This is, in our opinion, the most dramatic view, and if you're a photographer looking to catch the evening light, you'll find the most depth here.

From this first viewpoint you have several options of what to do next. If you are feeling adventurous, you can follow the path to the left across the headland all the way to the lighthouse. This walk will take you around 45 minutes to an hour. The concrete path is well maintained, but it can get steep in parts so does require some effort. You'll find plenty of clifftop spots where you can settle down and enjoy the view along the route.

We mentioned earlier that this is one of Skye's most-photographed landmarks, and it can get pretty busy, but don't let that put you off. Though there are often quite a few people there, it doesn't feel crowded, but like a gathering of like-minded people. You'll see campervans with their roofs popped, people sipping beers in camping chairs, photographers lining up their shots, and couples splayed out on rugs. There's a real buzz in the air!

Everyone has come to see the same thing: one of the UK's finest sunsets. As we shared in this joyful communal experience, we found ourselves wondering how different it must have been years ago, when perhaps the only people here for this stunning natural show were those few souls keeping watch in the lighthouse. As we watched the sun slip below the horizon, we felt a deep sense of appreciation that we were able to see it for ourselves. It's undoubtedly one of the best moments the UK has to offer.

Don't forget

This is an exposed clifftop in the far northwest of Scotland. Check the wind speed along with the weather – it can be brutal – and try to visit on a warm summer's day, if possible. And of course, as you're high up on the cliffs, you should be careful whatever the weather!

The 'Royal Bothy' hike

It's not every day that you get to stay in close proximity to a royal residence, but Gelder Shiel offers this unique experience. This bothy used to be a stable for a royal cottage, built in the grounds of Scotland's Balmoral Estate. Its renovation into a basic bothy has given it a new lease of life for bothyists. Its position on the bleak flanks of Lochnagar makes it a particularly special place to break up your hike near the foot of the mountain.

Time	few hours
Fitness	medium
Cost	free
Effort	medium
Equipment	required
Transport	best by car

Is this for me?

This is most certainly not the most comfortable adventure. If, like us, you tackle it in the winter, the hike leaves you very exposed to the Scottish elements, and once you get there the wooden beds of the bothy can be uncomfortable even for the most solid sleepers.

What this adventure is guaranteed to deliver, however, is a real sense of isolation. Its position, bedded in a vast moorland plain, framed by snow-capped mountains, gives the so-called 'Royal Bothy' a unique feeling of cosy sanctuary. This is what made the adventure for us; with only a short hike we felt like we were genuinely able to escape the noise of our everyday lives and appreciate the wild beauty of the Cairngorms.

The adventure

First things first: you'll need to check the weather before setting out. As mentioned, you are completely exposed to the elements for the entire hike, so plan accordingly and ensure you bring enough layers. If you are planning on staying the night in the bothy, then you'll also need to carry camping equipment such as sleeping bags, mats, a cooking stove, matches, ample food, water and snacks.

The hike starts at the carpark in the small village of Crathie, which you can reach either by car or on the 203 bus. Head out of the village on the tarmac road which passes by the old Post Office. It will turn into a well-maintained track running past a collection of lovely little houses. After the houses, take a left into the woods, and you'll soon be leaving behind any signs of civilization.

The landscape opens up after half a mile of trekking through the trees, revealing sweeping views towards Lochnagar. After only 45 minutes or so of following the track, you'll reach the bothy, which will most likely come as a very welcome break from the elements. As you open the old doors to enter you will immediately be met with a sense of cosiness. Gelder Shiel is a larger bothy than most. Its size has allowed it to be used by large groups of hikers since its conversion from a stable. It was a long-standing lifesaving haven for climbers tackling the surrounding mountains in the colder months, who would depend on each other's body heat to keep warm. Thankfully, modernization has included adding new insulation, making it much more comfortable.

The interior includes three bunk beds, a small table, chairs, a couple of small windows and the fireplace. A small but mighty stove heats the whole bothy with ease once it's roaring. There are also a few luxuries most bothies lack, such as running water and a basic hole-in-the-ground toilet. On one of the windowsills we found a dram of whisky, three cigarettes, some matches and a deck of cards. Giving back like this is tradition in bothy culture, so if you do have any surplus supplies when you're leaving the bothy, be sure to leave them for the next guests. That said, although it's common for provisions to be left, you absolutely shouldn't count on them being there!

Immediately opposite Gelder Shiel's front door is the royal cottage. Even now, members of the royal family make impromptu visits, so depending on your luck you may cross paths with one of them. That would no doubt be a pretty surreal experience, all things considered!

From the bothy you have a few options. You can either head up Conachcraig or Lochnagar for their drama-filled vistas, using the bothy as your base, or if you're short on time just head back the way you came to Balmoral.

Don't forget

As with most bothies, this is a remote adventure and you can often be subjected to rapid changes in the weather. It is also very unlikely you will have a phone signal. It is better to be over-prepared for this adventure, for your own safety. We'd definitely recommend taking the extra precaution of telling one or two people your plans.

As always, don't forget the Bothy Code (see page 223). It's a simple set of common-sense rules to help maintain the bothies for everyone. Let's ensure that everyone can enjoy the bothy tradition for generations to come.

As you stand watching the sun set over the ocean on the white sands of Iona's dramatic north coast, you'll feel a million miles from life's stresses. Cars aren't allowed here without a permit, and with only 177 residents, you'll find it easy to slip into the island's slow pace of life. Time spent in the spectacular natural surroundings of Iona will stay with you for a long while.

Time multi-day

Fitness low

Cost affordable

Effort medium

Equipment none

Transport best by car

The Inner Hebrides, Scotland

A night on Iona

Is it for me?

If you are looking to get in on one of the UK's best-kept secrets and aren't afraid to travel for it, then this might be the place for you. And with two nice hotels (St Columba and Argyll) on the island, plus a few campsites, staying the night can be as comfortable or adventurous as you like.

The only thing that elevates the Iona experience from entry-level difficulty to slightly more advanced is actually getting there. You have to take a small passenger ferry from the far side of Mull, so if you're coming from the mainland, you'll need to be prepared for a fair bit of driving and then at least two ferries.

The adventure

Located a mile off the east coast of the Isle of Mull, Iona is a tiny island with a truly unique atmosphere. Known as Scotland's cradle of Christianity, it is steeped in history, and visiting feels like taking a journey back in time.

Getting there is your first real challenge. From the small village of Fionnphort on Mull's west coast, the ferry takes around 20 minutes. You can buy tickets either online or at the terminal, which has a carpark and is on the 96 and 496 bus routes. Even before you set foot on the ferry to Iona, its unique beauty captures your attention. You can see its entire length from Mull, its profile punctuated by a series of pretty little buildings leading to a disproportionately large church. This is Iona Abbey – but we'll come to that in a moment.

On disembarking, you leave behind any semblance of 'mainland mentality' and settle straight into island pace, the calmness of Iona washing over you with immediate effect. The seafront cottages, tiny post office and breathtaking beach make for a memorable first glimpse of this secluded community.

When we visited the island, we based ourselves at Iona Pods, a basic but comfortable glampsite in a gorgeous setting. Each wooden pod comes complete with a bed, fridge and electric hob inside and benches outside. Other on-site facilities include a very clean shower block, washing-up area and washing machine room.

Tip: Book ahead for an excellent dinner at St Columba Hotel; its lovely staff, gorgeous views of Mull and modern Scottish fusion cuisine all make eating here a real pleasure.

Once you're settled in, it's time to explore. In all honesty, there aren't a whole lot of conventional 'attractions' on Iona. Rather, visitors come here just to roam the island. That said, it's worth making time to visit Iona Craft Shop. Not only can you refuel here with a delicious cup of coffee, but you can also hire a bike – cycling is a great option for zipping around the island. The shop also sells a whole host of locally sourced craft items, including beautiful knitwear made from Iona wool.

The island's biggest draw is its extraordinary coastline, with its four beautiful white-sand beaches – you'll find it hard to believe that some of them are even in the UK. For us the pick of the bunch was North End – which, as the name suggests, is located at the island's northernmost end. With views over the Atlantic Ocean, Treshnish Isles, Mull and more, this beach is the perfect place to while away an afternoon. Stay to watch the sunset if you can.

Even if you're not a history buff, it's worth seeing Iona Abbey. St Columba founded a monastery here way back in the sixth century, making Iona one of the oldest Christian centres in western Europe. The abbey itself is among the UK's most important religious buildings. It rises up much taller than anything else on Iona, infusing the whole area with a sense of mysticism and deep history.

A trip to Iona offers a unique UK experience, combining a sense of seclusion and stunning nature with enough comforts to make it a fairly accessible adventure. We really would have liked to have stayed longer, but if like us you are tight on time, it's still worth visiting even for a day trip or a one-night stay.

Don't forget

Pre-book your accommodation and dinner to avoid disappointment, especially at peak times. There is only one shop on the island, a Little Spar, and once it's closed you have nowhere else to go for food other than the two restaurants.

Wales

Size 8192 square miles (21,218 sq km)

National parks 3 (covering 20% of land area)

UNESCO World Heritage Sites 4

Highest peak Yr Wyddfa (Snowdon; 1085m)

Coastline over 1680 miles (2700 km)

Waterfalls over 75

There is a real freedom to sea-kayaking, the vastness of the ocean making the possibilities feel endless. The Pembrokeshire Coast National Park is one of the UK's best destinations for this activity, with beautiful bays, numerous little coves to dip in and out of, towering cliffs and the chance to spot seals and porpoises along the way making for varied and exciting routes.

Time	few hours / full day
Fitness	medium
Cost	affordable
Effort	medium
Equipment	required
Transport	best by car

Pembrokeshire, Wales

Sea-kayaking the Pembrokeshire coast

Is this for me?

Though you don't need to paddle the entire coast, kayaking does require a certain degree of upper body strength. And though you should be wearing a life jacket anyway, we'd advise against this adventure if you're not a confident swimmer.

If neither of these things puts you off however, we really couldn't recommend it more as a means to explore the coast. Kayaking has no parallels when it comes to freedom, allowing you to access hard-to-reach coves and serene stretches of coastline that you might otherwise not ever come across.

While the freedom of exploring at your own pace is something we feel adds to the adventure, there are also companies that offer guided tours for those less confident in the sea. This is also a good option if you're using public transport, as you can take a bus to St Davids or Solva and they will pick you up from there. This is a much more expensive activity than simply renting the kayak by itself.

The adventure

The Pembrokeshire Coast National Park is one of three national parks in Wales, and has certainly the most stunning stretch of coastline. Honestly, with its vast, beautiful and bizarre rock formations, it has to be in contention for the most dramatic coastline in the UK – enormous cliffs and sea stacks pepper the ocean, the beaches are long and the caves are deep! Exploring it at water level gives you a chance to get up close and personal with the area's unusual geology.

There are plenty of places to rent kayaks in Pembrokeshire. We recommend TYF in St Davids, a picturesque little town west of the national park. They're an outdoor adventure company specializing in coastal adventure, with surfing, coasteering, rock climbing and sea-kayaking equipment. Group trips with a professional are also available.

As we wanted to explore at our own pace, we simply rented individual kayaks (plus handy dry bags for storing all our stuff). We also stocked up at the local bakery/deli opposite TYF.

Tip: TYF rents out temporary kayak racks for your car, which they can also quickly and easily install for you. We really recommend this option, as it means there's no limit to where you can start your adventure!

All kitted out, it's time to head to Porthclais, a small port where the River Alun meets the sea. It's under 10 minutes' drive west along the coast from St Davids, and makes a great launching spot as it's so close to several cool little hidden bays. Head to the carpark, from where it's a short walk with your kayaks down the estuary to the sea. We recommend doing this adventure at low tide as it will reveal plenty of hidden coves.

Once you're in the water, head left (east) and begin to slip into the rhythm of paddling. It won't be long before you understand why people bang on about sea-kayaking on this stretch of coast. The water is a gorgeous blue, and to one side dramatic cliffs rise up beside you, while to the other – nothing but open sea. The kayak is small but mighty. Use it to slip easily between rocks and into little coves. Around every corner is a new hidden inlet or beach, so keep going until you find one that catches your eye.

If you are looking for a scenic spot to stop for lunch, then paddle past St Non's chapel and Caerfai Bay (a wedge-shaped sandy bay with turquoise water). You will reach a stretch of water between the mainland and a tiny, rocky island called Penpleidiau. The water at low tide becomes really shallow and sheltered from the wider ocean by the island, making it a great spot to see white stones, seaweed and tiny fish.

It's here, on the mainland just across from the island, that you will find a secluded little pebble bay hidden away from the world, out of the breeze and home to warm water – the perfect place to hop out of your kayaks to eat, sunbathe, swim and explore the surrounding rocks.

Don't forget

If you are lucky enough to do this on a sunny day, make sure you rent the kayaks for long enough to relax and take in this experience.

Hiking Cadair Idris and wild swimming in Llyn Cau

A vast, crystal-clear lake in the crater of a spectacular Welsh mountain, Llyn Cau is, without a doubt, one of the most epic wild swimming spots in the UK. Rock faces swathed in green rise 400 metres above the water on each side. Truly, there is absolutely nowhere else like it in the UK.

Time	few hours
Fitness	medium
Cost	free
Effort	high
Equipment	none
Transport	best by car

Is this for me?

There are two halves to this adventure. First, you'll walk to the crater lake of Llyn Cau, then you'll hike to the summit on Cadair Idris. If you are short on time, with kids or don't fancy the whole excursion, then you can skip the summit, though of course even hiking to the lake is reasonably demanding. Fit people will be able to complete the ascent to Cadair Idris via Llyn Cau in around two and a half hours, and descend within one and a half. Remember – Cadair Idris is a mountain. It starts steep, and only gets steeper towards the summit!

As with most places in the countryside, travelling by car is the easiest and fastest option. However, it is possible to catch a bus from Machynlleth to Minffordd, from where you can start the hike.

The adventure

Cadair Idris is an 893-metre-tall peak in Snowdonia National Park. It is a beauty of a mountain, famous for the crater lake halfway up. There are plenty of routes up the mountain, from which we chose the quickest (and steepest), the Minffordd Path.

The nearest train stations, Machynlleth and Barmouth, are each a bus journey away. The easiest and most time-efficient way of getting there is by car; if that's an option for you, we recommend simply chucking your swimming stuff, some good boots, snacks and water in the boot, and making a beeline for Dol Idris carpark.

From there, take the obvious path towards the mountain until you reach the stairs cut into the stone. The Minffordd Path is a pretty punishing trail. Though, whichever one you take, you'll soon find the gradient increasing every few steps. As you wind along the path hugging the forest, you'll ask yourself if it'll get easier. Much to the relief of your tired legs, it will, as the path then flattens slightly – this is the sign you're close to the lake.

Take the small path to your right towards the mountain crater. You'll know you've reached Llyn Cau when your jaw drops. Between the gorgeous, prismatic lake and the enormous mountains cradling it, you won't know where to look.

The lake is home to many local legends. It is said that if you sleep on the slopes of Llyn Cau, you'll awaken as either a madman or a poet! We're here to swim, though, so the so-called 'bottomless' lake is a bigger risk. Rest assured, the only real danger here is the cold; the shadow cast by the mountain and the deep waters combine to make this one of the coldest places we've ever swum! With this in mind, make sure you don't swim alone, especially if you're a fairly novice wild swimmer. The cold will take your breath away, which can be dangerous if you're not used to it.

After you've finished taking in Llyn Cau, head back to the main path. You'll find the walk to the summit an excellent way to warm up, and the ever-changing views will distract you from any lingering shivers. The summit is high above the lake, giving you a bird's-eye view of where you were just swimming, and it's easy to imagine how miniscule you must have looked to people up here. And the 360-degree views might give you some clue as to why the mountain is called a 'giant's seat'!

Don't forget

Make sure you keep a keen eye on the weather. Conditions can change rapidly, sometimes landing ill-prepared ramblers in trouble. Make sure you have made adequate preparations, bring a waterproof (even in summer) – and, of course, don't forget your swimming costume!

Powys, Wales

Camping in Bannau Brycheiniog

This is a one-night adventure all about freedom. You'll camp under the stars, explore the mountainous scenery of the Brecon Beacons, and cross briefly over the border into England as you paddle your way along the Wye. By its end, you'll feel both refreshed and better connected to this sensational part of the UK.

Time multi-day

Fitness low

Cost affordable

Effort medium

Equipment required

Transport car required

Is this for me?

This adventure is for those who like to get stuck in and feel disconnected from urban life for a while. It is a two-day experience that takes you from the heights of the Beacons to the fast-flowing waters of the Wye Valley.

Camping's not for everyone; if you like your creature comforts, then this may not be the one for you. However, if you're on the fence, we urge you to give it a go. There really is no better feeling than unzipping your tent or opening your campervan door and stepping straight out into the landscapes of Bannau Brycheiniog (formerly Brecon Beacons National Park) – it really is an incomparable way to start your day.

The adventure

Bannau Brycheiniog National Park is a 350-square-mile (906-square-km) area in the east of Wales. It's known for its stunning landscapes, making for a great retreat in the south of the UK. For our two-day, one-night adventure we decided to start here and head for the Wye Valley, stopping off at a campsite on the way.

Preparation is quite straightforward. Book a pitch, pack your car with everything you need for a night under the stars and your kayaking trip...

Once in the national park, you're spoiled for choice when it comes to places to explore. If waterfalls are your thing, the 5½-mile (9 km) Four Waterfalls Walk is a great place to start. If sitting on your bum is more appealing, try driving the Black Mountain Road, which twists and turns through some spectacularly scenic landscapes. This adventure is all about impulsivity, so judge it on the weather and what you fancy on the day. In our case, we were a little short on time when we arrived, so we decided to head straight for Pen y Fan. We'd climbed it several times before (see page 184), but just by taking a different route up we had a completely new experience.

After descending the mountain we headed to our campsite. Bannau Brycheiniog is home to lots of 'nearly wild' campsites. These privately owned areas of land are both uncrowded and unbothered.

We booked a spot at Pwllyn Farm, a scenic 15-minute drive from the small town of Brecon. The owner is welcoming, giving you plenty of options for where to pitch – he'll let you survey the whole area before choosing. The campsite has a sheltered communal area with all the necessities like washing-up facilities, showers, charging points and cooking hobs. The rest of the farm strikes a great balance between well-kept and wild, and is surrounded by beautiful mountain views.

In the morning, we packed up and made a beeline for the Wye Valley, where the River Wye runs for 250 miles (402 km) through Wales to the Severn Estuary. After an hour's drive we reached Kerne Bridge, a small town over the border in Herefordshire. It's home to one of the best launch spots onto the river, with a nearby carpark which makes a perfect base for operations. The river has concrete steps for easy entry to the water, and a converted vintage fire engine nearby which sells snacks and drinks. All in all, if you're going to kayak anywhere on the Wye, make it Kerne Bridge!

From Kerne Bridge the river flows through glorious countryside down towards Symonds Yat. A village straddling the river, it's best known for Symonds Yat Rock, which is not only the most famous viewpoint over the River Wye but also home to an Iron Age hillfort. You can reach Symonds Yat within half a day, though wherever you decide to stop, you'll then have the challenge of getting your kayak back to Kerne Bridge.

If you are able to rent an inflatable kayak, this will enable you to pack it down, which is great for hitching a ride back, but if you're not comfortable with hitchhiking or have a non-inflatable kayak, you'll need to make other plans! Most canoe hire companies offer a drop off or pick up service.

Once back at the Kerne Bridge launch point, it's time to reward yourself. There's only one place for that... the converted fire engine! It's called The Paddle Café, and it offers fresh coffee, baked treats, sandwiches and beers with a river view. We found the food just as memorable as the location, and made a note of their bespoke picnic hampers (book in advance) for our next trip.

Don't forget

The Wye leg of this adventure comes with some specific dangers. The water runs rapidly, and has some strong undercurrents. You should do your best to not risk your own safety while out on the water. Life jackets and helmets are non-negotiable, as you could capsize at any moment; they can be rented from most local canoe and kayak hire companies.

Tip: For this adventure we took an inflatable kayak that we rented from Decathlon. We chose this because it packs down neatly into our car boot. You can always rent canoes and kayaks along the river, though, if that fits your plans better – there are a few different options in Kerne Bridge.

If you're a fan of outdoor cooking, fresh ingredients and rugged coastal landscapes, then this may well be the adventure for you. It is an afternoon full of surprises, and one that will not only engage you throughout but also teach you skills to take forward into future adventures. You'll come away with a whole new appreciation for some of the rich bounty the natural world has to offer.

Time	few hours
Fitness	low
Cost	affordable
Effort	low
Equipment	none
Transport	best by car

Pembrokeshire, Wales

Coastal foraging in Pembrokeshire

Is this for me?

Whether you're a fairly experienced forager or just interested in giving it a try, an afternoon spent with Craig Evans will open your mind to a whole world of possibilities. The value of this adventure is not just the connection with nature, but even more so the chance to spend time with and learn from someone so knowledgeable.

This is a really easy adventure in terms of physicality – when we tried it, it was alongside several people over the age of 60 and a couple of young-uns. A good one for all the family, especially as under-16s go free. Beach wheelchairs are also available upon request.

The adventure

'You'll never look at the beach in the same way again' is the promise Craig Evans, founder of Coastal Foraging, makes before he takes you out on one of his food-based experiences on the Pembrokeshire coast. A bold claim, but one that he will immediately set about proving.

Along with his golden retriever, Llew, Craig takes groups out along the southern Welsh coastline to show them just how incredibly diverse and rich in edible ingredients that environment is. He offers a variety of trips with a range of times and focuses. The most popular is the Classic course – the one we tried. Like most of the experiences, it takes place within 20 minutes' drive of the famous seaside town of Tenby. Craig will share the exact meeting place the week before, and if you arrive by public transport you will receive a discount. You can then jump in his car for a lift to any subsequent foraging locations.

When we went in August, our Classic course kicked off in a small forest. Craig showed us how to identify and harvest big juicy Welsh oyster mushrooms, immediately opening our eyes to an abundance of wild ingredients we'd previously overlooked. From the forest we travelled a short way along the coast, hiking through more woodland to the main arena... the beach.

To kick off the coastal foraging, you're given an empty bucket. As you traverse the beach, that bucket slowly fills with edible treasures: soft shell clams and cockles pulled up from beneath the sand; crabs and prawns from under the rocks; wild samphire picked from the cliff face. You will leave no stone unturned, almost literally.

Once you are satisfied with your fresh Welsh finds you hike back along the beach, hugging the cliff line to reach a small spot out of the wind where Craig sets about starting a small fire to cook your foraged feast. This is, as I'm sure you can imagine, the most satisfying part of the adventure. With Llew watching on longingly, Craig begins to fry up wild garlic with the oyster mushrooms, the delicious smells wafting across the sand as he adds all your foraged finds to create a deliciously fresh seafood broth.

The adventure culminates with you sitting on the rocks overlooking the sea, enjoying your meal, and appreciating the beauty and bounty of the Welsh coast. There is something very cool about a food-based experience that is, end to end, entirely natural: fresh ingredients, open fire and an extraordinary setting.

Craig captures the spontaneous spirit of this adventure by saying that you can never predict the menu, as you never know exactly what you will find. Foraging is all about what nature has for you that day. Each experience is unique, a dive into the unknown, and that is where the excitement lies.

Don't forget

Bring a snack and some water. While you'll feast at the end of the day, the course can take anywhere from six to eight hours, so it's best to bring a little something to give you an energy boost along the way. What's more, this is Wales and the weather can be extremely changeable, so layer up and bring a waterproof.

There are no regular courses catering for vegetarians, but you can opt for a course focused on plant life. Note that you need a minimum party of six for a bespoke course like this.

There is no better way to absorb the scale and beauty of the eastern tip of Bannau Brycheiniog than to climb Pen y Fan. It is a short, fairly easy hike with a wealth of incredible viewpoints along the way, which gives you ample opportunity to appreciate the majesty of Wales.

Time	few hours
Fitness	medium
Cost	free
Effort	medium
Equipment	none
Transport	best by car

Powys, Wales

Climbing Pen y Fan

Is this for me?

If you are looking for a spectacular mountain that is relatively easy to climb, then this is most certainly the adventure for you.

There are four established paths up Pen y Fan that vary in time and difficulty, meaning it has a good spread of options for all abilities. We opted for the easiest one, often known as the Storey Arms trail due to its starting point near the Storey Arms Outdoor Centre. This is the most direct and gentle route to the top, making it achievable for people of all ages.

As with most Welsh mountains, though, the weather conditions are unpredictable. So if you're looking for guaranteed clear views, this probably isn't the adventure for you.

The adventure

Part of Bannau Brycheiniog, Pen y Fan is the highest mountain in south Wales. It is also only a few hours' drive from London, making it a great option for city dwellers looking for their fix of fresh air and adventure. The catch here is that, of course, this also makes it very popular. It can get pretty busy, especially at the weekend. To really make the most of this experience and avoid the crowds, we recommend a sunrise hike, as most others will still be in bed!

Preparation for this adventure is pretty straightforward: check the weather and dress accordingly, with sturdy boots recommended, then make sure you've got plenty of water and some snacks. We took breakfast and a thermos of tea for the top, as we were setting out so early. That said, at peak times there is a van in the main carpark serving tea, coffee and breakfast baps, so you can grab something here if you don't want to carry much.

The route starts at the newly expanded Pont ar Daf carpark (free for National Trust members), which is around 10 minutes' drive from the nearby town of Brecon. If you'd rather use public transport, your best bet is the T4 bus from Brecon, which stops by the carpark.

From here, you simply follow the very obvious path over the first bridge, then up the mountainside. This route to the top of Pen y Fan is only about two miles long and is on a gradual gradient, so it's not too testing. We managed to hike to the 480-metre summit in around an hour and a half, which is fairly good going. If you are a little less used to hiking or have kids with you we would recommend leaving about an extra half hour each way.

Heading up, the conditions will of course dictate your views, but on a clear day the surrounding landscapes quite quickly become spectacular. If you do get lucky, from the top you will be able to see a variety of sharp ridges cutting across the horizon, alongside rolling valleys, intricate tributaries and mountain lakes.

Once you reach the top we recommend spending a bit of time just taking it all in, appreciating the scale of this place and enjoying feeling so small and insignificant in comparison. The summit is actually a plateau rather than a dramatic crag, so it's quite easy to explore once you're up there.

From there you have the option to follow your steps back down, or to continue on along some of the other routes, the hardest and no doubt most epic of which takes you along the dramatic Horseshoe Ridge. If you are after extending the adventure and indeed taking it up a few notches, then we highly recommend this.

Don't forget

Pack extra layers for the summit. Even if it's a warm day at the foot of the mountain, it can be quite cool and windy at the top.

Discovering the Llŷn Peninsula

The Llŷn Peninsula, or the 'Arm of Wales', is a sliver of land on the edge of Snowdonia reaching out into the Irish Sea. What you will find here is quite different from the rest of Wales. Often compared to Cornwall, this small peninsula is packed full of tiny coves, epic cliffs, sandy beaches and coastal villages, and over 60 square miles (155 square km) is classed as an Area of Outstanding Natural Beauty.

Time multi-day

Fitness low

Cost affordable

Effort medium

Equipment none

Transport car required

Is this for me?

If you are looking for a corner of the UK that is beautiful and peaceful, then the Llŷn Peninsula may well be for you. Rock stacks, sweeping sandy beaches, water sports and windblown cliffs make it an incredible example of the drama and variety of Wales' beautiful coastline.

Due to its location in the northwestern extremity of Wales, getting there from the vast majority of UK locations will involve quite a drive, so it's not the best adventure for those without a car. But as with most remote locations, you will be rewarded for your efforts; the sweeping seascapes and gorgeous Welsh scenery are, for the most part, relatively uncrowded.

The adventure

The Llŷn Peninsula is perhaps one of the country's best-kept secrets. Often overshadowed by its near neighbour Snowdonia, the peninsula sneaks under the radar, but its white sands, water sports and picturesque villages make it a top-tier destination for a coastal adventure.

We visited on a three-day road trip, but there is plenty to do if you want to spend longer here. Conversely, if you have a trip planned to Snowdonia or Anglesey, a day trip to the peninsula is certainly worthwhile.

Extending around 30 miles (48 km) into the Irish Sea, this thin strip of land is bordered by a collection of incredible beaches. Their sheer quantity and variety mean that, by heading just slightly off the beaten track, you can earn a beach all to yourself. If you have a few days to spend here, hop between a few.

Situated halfway along the north coast of the peninsula, the beach in the gorgeous little village of Porthdinllaen is tucked away behind a golf course. Due to its idyllic waters and picturesque buildings, this National Trust-owned beach can actually get quite busy, but get there for an early morning stroll and you'll have a blissfully quiet time. Once the sand starts filling up, retire for a pint and a bite at the Tŷ Coch Inn, which lives up to its moniker of 'arguably the best pub in Wales'.

To step further off the beaten track, make a beeline for Traeth Penllech, just 20 minutes west by car. At low tide this gorgeous sandy beach stretches for miles, with rock pools at either end and even a small waterfall in its middle. With views looking out to the west, it's the perfect spot to cook up an alfresco dinner and marvel at the sunset. Make sure you head there with all your supplies, then build up a small fire and get cooking! And, of course, ensure you leave no trace when you pack up.

Another 20-minute drive down the coast, Traeth Porthor – also known as 'Whistling Sands' due to the sound the sand makes when you step on it – is one of the Llŷn Peninsula's most popular beaches, which means it has some handy facilities including a great little café. We'd suggest using the area as a base, then taking the small coastal pathway to the left of the main beach. Soon the trail will split in two; take the lower track to head off the beaten path, and closer to the rocky beaches that line this stretch of coast. Low tide reveals an intricate network of rock pools, prime for exploring.

Right at the western tip of the peninsula is Traeth Aberdaron, a long strip of sand which is perfect for your typical beach day of lazing about, swimming and walking. If you're feeling a little more adventurous, though, you could also use it as a launch point for several water-based activities including surfing, windsurfing or sea-kayaking; you can hire equipment in the town of Pwllheli, around 30 minutes' drive away

If you fancy getting a good dose of fresh air while exploring a lesser-known part of the UK, then the Llŷn Peninsula is definitely worth considering. It's a great place to blow away the cobwebs, and reconnect with the UK's wild nature.

Don't forget

If you're planning to cook at any of the beaches, it's probably most convenient to pick up supplies at the supermarket in Pwllheli on the south coast – the only large store on the peninsula – or in Porthmadog.

Wild swimming at Wolf's Leap

While away an afternoon exploring this gem of a valley – swimming in its hidden pools, lazing on the grass verges and simply watching the day go by. A visit to this oasis of calm will leave you feeling refreshed and revitalized.

Time few hours / full day

Fitness low

Cost free

Effort low

Equipment none

Transport car required

Is this for me?

As spots in east Wales go, this is pretty remote and requires a car or bike to get to. If you aren't afraid of that commitment, then a trip to this hidden corner of the UK is a perfect adventure. A plunge in one of the pools at Wolf's Leap is the perfect way to reboot yourself; something about the steep valley sides and natural waterfalls is almost prehistoric.

But be warned: these waters can be fairly dangerous. And whatever the weather, they're guaranteed to be ice cold... Of course, you don't have to swim; even if you only dip your toes in, you will still love the beauty of this place.

The adventure

Wolf's Leap consists of a series of deep pools of varying sizes at the bottom of a narrow gorge along the River Irfon, Llanwrtyd. This section of the river runs through an isolated and beautiful valley only accessible via a single-track road that runs its length. The valley is peppered with rocky outcrops and hill streams that run down its sides to feed the Irfon, making for an epic setting.

Preparation relies on the time of year you are planning to visit. We went on a frigid January day and needed a wardrobe's worth of extra warm clothing. We knew we'd need it after we got out of the water, which was, needless to say, very very cold. Due to the wet winter weather we also needed our hiking boots to navigate the slippery slopes of the valley. It's certainly easier to visit in the summer months, when you'll only need a solid pair of shoes and your swimming gear, plus food and a picnic rug on the grassy banks of the river.

Getting here is fairly straightforward but takes some persistence due to its isolated location above the village of Abergwesyn. Once you make it to Wolf's Leap, follow the track along the valley and park up in one of the little sidings. Then, get changed and make your way to the river in search of a swimmable pool.

At the foot of the valley the grass flattens out, making for a great spot to lay down your rug and set up camp. Here there are several swimming spots of varying depth, some of them quite deep plunge pools, all beautifully clear – but with arctic water! On a warm summer's day this is the perfect spot to cool down.

If you have time after your swim, we recommend following some of the narrow sheep tracks up the sides of the valley. Once you've reached the top, you'll be treated to stunning views of the sweeping landscape. It makes for a great way to round things off.

To extend the adventure, consider staying at nearby Hergest Lee, situated in the tiny hamlet of Burlingjobb, near Presteigne and Kington. This handcrafted cabin is one of the UK's most unique hideaways, a beautifully designed spot about 40 minutes' drive from the valley. The larger of the two buildings, the lean-to, is one of the most memorable places we've ever stayed. The modern architecture together with the carefully curated interiors which combine mid-century, antique and modern pieces creates a space that feels effortlessly cool. The earthy tones and use of natural materials, meanwhile, lend a feeling of connection to the surrounding nature. The efforts of owners and designers Paul and Rachel Gent haven't gone unnoticed.

Don't forget

The time of year and the weather will dictate how dangerous the pools are. In the wetter months the river can get pretty fierce; this may result in most or all of the pools being unswimmable. If this is the case, you can still walk downstream to a couple of much shallower, calmer options – that's exactly what we did on a slightly hairy midwinter's day.

Hiking Y Garn

On this trip, you'll feel as though you're standing on the shoulders of giants. The fantastic beast of Snowdonia is so large it is humbling, its sheer scale awe-inspiring. Peaks fade into hazy purples on the horizon; mountain lakes gleam like sapphires; and, on clear days, the sea shimmers in the distance. Without a doubt, the views from the summit of Y Garn are up there with the best in Snowdonia.

Time few hours

Fitness medium

Cost free

Effort high

Equipment none

Transport best by car

Is this for me?

Snowdonia has a reputation for gruelling, intense hikes, but Y Garn manages to give you the views without too much hard work. You can reach the summit in under an hour and a half, and when you make it to the top, you'll be treated to 360-degree views of the surrounding national park.

That said, you are still climbing a mountain, and so will need a degree of fitness. You will also have to do a little bit of scrambling on loose rocks, which means it might not be suitable for everyone.

This adventure is definitely easier if you have a car, but there is an infrequent T10 TrawsCymru bus service between Bethesda and Capel Curig. It stops at Ogwen, from where you could start your hike.

The adventure

Located in north Wales' Snowdonia National Park, Y Garn is the tenth-highest mountain in Wales. It's one of the Welsh 3000s, a group of mountains over 3000 feet (914 metres) tall, standing proud at 3106 feet (947 metres).

Preparation for this hike is the same as most. You need a good pair of sturdy walking boots and plenty of layers. You'll need a bag with snacks, water and a thermos of hot tea – trust us, the tea is non-negotiable if you are planning on attacking Y Garn in the colder months. On that note, this adventure is suitable year-round. Summer brings luscious green scenes and winter creates snow-speckled spectacle. Even in the worst conditions of fog and rain, which is the sort of weather in which we tackled it, this hike is still worth it. As long as you avoid extreme weather conditions by checking your weather app ahead of time, you'll be OK.

To get there, if driving, make your way to the Ogwen Centre, where you can park your car for a small fee. From there, set off on the marked path southwards towards the shoreline of Llyn Llydaw. This mountain lake is a perfect vista with which to start your adventure. Head around the shoreline to the ominous-sounding Devil's Kitchen, a vast ravine looming over you, which is your path to the summit. As expected from a ravine, the path up is rocky and loose in places. You have to watch your footing the entire way up – lower your centre of gravity against the rock face for extra stability.

Your reward for conquering this section is the views back down over Llyn Llydaw. While you pause to admire the panorama, take the opportunity for a quick pitstop, with some water and a short sit down.

Once you've recharged a bit, continue up to Llyn y Cwm, where you turn right and continue on up for just under a mile further to the summit of Y Garn. The walk to the summit isn't as intense as the Devil's Kitchen, so enjoy yourself. Once you reach the end of this short and intense hike, you'll find the wild beauty of Snowdonia spread out below you. And with the walk only being an hour and a half in total, you might just spot your next adventure from here in time to head back down and make your way over!

This part of the UK is unlike any other. Here you'll find some of the most spectacular scenes in the British Isles, and if you enjoy water-based activities then you won't find any better place to go. A single trip to Pembrokeshire will leave you asking yourself – why haven't I been here before?

Time	multi-day
Fitness	low
Cost	affordable
Effort	medium
Equipment	none
Transport	car required

Pembrokeshire, Wales

Exploring the Pembrokeshire coastline

Is this for me?

The Pembrokeshire coastline is in a league of its own, with innumerable variations of cliffs, beaches and rock formations. For the watersport-inclined, you shouldn't even ask the question – this adventure is for you. For everyone else, this area is so jam-packed with options that we're confident there'll be something for you.

The only question is, how long should you stay? You could easily spend just an afternoon exploring, but you'll wish you had more time.

The adventure

The Pembrokeshire Coast National Park is one of three national parks in Wales. It's home to one of the most stunning, dramatic stretches of coastline in the UK, dotted with bizarre rock formations. Think sea stacks, enormous cliffs, unreal beaches, deep caves and limestone arches. We found ourselves in a constant state of amazement while exploring.

It's up to you how you prepare for this adventure. If, like us, you are going for a road trip, then you might want to factor in time for impulsive stops. You could stop almost anywhere here and see a view worth soaking in, but there are three spots which stood out to us in particular.

Green Bridge and Elegug Stacks

A clifftop hike is a great way to kick off your Pembrokeshire adventure. These rock formations are icons of the region. The Green Bridge is an extraordinary natural arch of rock reaching out into the ocean. As you walk along the coast path, you'll pass several more unusual rock formations. The Elegug Stacks, known for their nesting guillemots, are every bit as awesome as the bridge.

> **Tip: The postcode for the carpark is not entirely accurate. Follow it, and you'll find a handwritten sign telling you that Google is wrong, and giving directions to the right place! This route will take you past a small chapel, and through a military firing range. Don't worry, it's safe the majority of the time, and you'll be warned when it isn't!**

Barafundle Bay

Far from secret, the extraordinary Barafundle Bay is often voted one of the best beaches in Britain. What makes it so special? Well, to us visiting Barafundle felt like stepping onto the pages of a storybook. We half expected to see a longship making landfall in the small bay, framed by pine trees and bracken-covered dunes.

There are two different routes to take from the carpark, around half a mile away. The first is faster and more popular, as it leads you along the coastal path. We prefer the second, which goes through the forest and the sand dunes instead, and is rarely busy. If you take this less-walked path first, you can leave via the more conventional route for a lovely walking loop!

This beautiful bay, shielded from winds and currents by the surrounding pine trees, is a great place to hang out. If you're not usually one for outdoor swimming, the bay's natural protection makes it a great place to try!

Hidden sunset spot

Our final recommendation comes from a local tip. We asked around for a spot to watch the sunset, and were advised to make our way down to the busy beach at Whitesands – then carry on along the coastal path, heading west past the campsite.

By hugging the shoreline for about 15 minutes, we were able to completely avoid the crowds, lulled by the sound of the sea lapping against the rocks. At this point we came to the rocky headland we had been told about, and scrambled a short way down to a fairly flat section. Then we picked the perfect spot – down by the water, out of the breeze and facing west. With our backs against the rocks, we watched the sun set over the ocean. We got the chance to enjoy this special moment all to ourselves, thanks to local knowledge.

Don't forget

The best places to go aren't always the easiest or most well advertised, so always ask around for tips!

Northern Ireland

Size 5530 square
miles (14,330 sq km)

**UNESCO World
Heritage Sites** 1

Highest peak Slieve
Donard (850m)

Beaches 35

Largest lake Lough
Neagh (19 miles long
and 9 miles wide /
31 km long and
14 km wide)

Sitting on your board looking back at the dramatic Northern Irish coast as you wait for a wave is a very cool feeling. It's not the situation that would first spring to mind when you think of a UK adventure, but surfing is perhaps Northern Ireland's best-kept secret. On this stretch of coast alone you'll have ample choice of spots to choose from, and won't have to fight over waves.

Time	few hours
Fitness	medium
Cost	affordable
Effort	high
Equipment	required
Transport	best by car

Causeway Coast, Northern Ireland

Surfing on the Causeway Coast

Is this for me?

Northern Ireland caters for all surfing abilities and appetites. Whether you are an intrigued newbie or an experienced seadog, there's a wave for everyone. For beginners, Benone's long sweeping beach with gentle waves and lots of space to spread out is ideal, while Runkerry's rip currents and shelving offer experienced surfers a hit of adrenaline. But one thing unites all these diverse spots... Let's just say that, if you're a fairweather surfer or averse to cold water, you might want to sit this one out!

Having a car gives you more options, but there are local buses and trains to the better-known spots, where you can also hire equipment or join a surf school. Benone Strand is Northern Ireland's first fully inclusive beach, offering beach wheelchairs and adapted surfboards, making it one of the best beaches for wheelchair users in the whole of the UK.

The adventure

We were really intrigued by the prospect of surfing in Northern Ireland. I think most people, like us, wouldn't instinctively put the two together in their minds! But when we headed out there, we quickly noticed that at almost every beach there would be at least one or two surfers bobbing on the horizon.

As it turns out, Northern Ireland is one of those places which in-the-know surfers head to for world-class waves without the crowds. With long, consistent breaks and beautiful beaches, the Causeway Coast is home to several great surfing spots. Sitting out on our boards, we certainly felt like we had been let in on a surfing community secret...

You don't need to worry about travelling with your gear, either, as there are plenty of different surf schools and shops where you can rent a board and wetsuit. If you do need to hire any kit or book a lesson, though, you should try and do this a couple of days in advance – and this goes double for the busier summer months. Then all you need is your swimming gear, a towel and some nice warm clothes to put on once you're out. A flask of tea or coffee wouldn't go amiss either, especially if you're sensitive to the cold.

There are several different beaches that have good surfable waves. You should pick one based on your ability, and depending on the weather and swells. We were still fairly new to the sport when we visited, though not complete beginners, so we opted for Portrush, 20 minutes' drive or a nine-minute train ride from Coleraine. The town's West Strand is one of Northern Ireland's best-known surf spots, particularly popular due to its consistent barrels – so if you're looking for somewhere to chat to clued-up locals and visitors, this is the place. The beach also has a surf school with great facilities and an even better reputation. We headed for neighbouring East Strand; its gentler waves are much easier for less-experienced surfers, and you can still make use of West Strand's facilities and classes.

Accessible Benone Strand, just half an hour's drive from Portrush, is arguably the most dramatically beautiful beach on the whole coast. It stretches a whopping seven miles and tends to have fairly small waves, so it's a great place for beginners to cut their teeth.

Between Portrush and Benone is Whiterocks, which as the name suggests is framed by white limestone cliffs and sea stacks. Anyone can enjoy the beauty of this spot and, weather allowing, there are waves for beginners and more experienced surfers alike. It's also a great spot for bodyboarders and sea-kayakers.

Don't forget

If it's been a while since you've surfed, it might be worth getting a refresher lesson before heading out by yourself. In our experience it takes a little while to get back in the swing of things, especially in unfamiliar waters, and a lesson can just speed that process up.

Driving the Causeway Coast

This journey will take you 130 miles (209 km) along Northern Ireland's wild Antrim and Derry/Londonderry coasts, where you can immerse yourself in the dramatic landscapes which shaped the region's evocative myths and legends. With plenty of sandy beaches, castles and caves en route, the Causeway Coastal Route is perhaps the UK's most underrated road trip.

Time multi-day

Fitness low

Cost affordable

Effort medium

Equipment none

Transport car required

Is this for me?

The beauty of all road trips is that they can be sculpted to your wants and needs, and this one is no different. With a plethora of different places to stop, from extraordinary beaches to waterfalls, whiskey distilleries to charming seaside towns, the Causeway Coastal Route has something for everyone. If you're after a break guaranteed to be bathed in sunshine, then this might not be the one for you. That said, we truly feel that come rain, wind or shine, this stretch of coastline delivers the drama.

The adventure

The most logical place to start this journey is from the route's southeastern tip in Belfast. It's well connected with airports on the UK mainland, but if like us you'd like to go plane-free, you'll find the ferry the most convenient option. We took the car ferry that departs from Liverpool Birkenhead, it takes eight hours to cross to Belfast. We got an overnight cabin complete with shower and comfy beds for a reasonable price. What's more, it means that when you get to the other side you just drive off and you're away – no fuss!

From Belfast, you drive north along the east coast, hugging the coastline as you work your way round the route. If you want to really explore this 130-mile (209-km) stretch of Northern Irish beauty, we recommend setting aside a week if possible.

With the timing of our own trip, we decided to make our first stop the Dark Hedges – just under an hour's drive from Belfast – in order to avoid the weekend rush. Essentially a single-track road in the middle of nowhere, it was made world famous when some scenes from *Game of Thrones* were filmed here. We're not usually fans of major tourist attractions, as hordes of people can ruin an experience, but if you get there first thing in the morning it's usually quiet enough that you can appreciate its magical atmosphere.

So what's all the fuss about? The Dark Hedges is a long road lined with beautiful old-growth beech trees. Over the centuries they've grown together, entwining to create a natural tunnel, which feels like nothing so much as the entrance to some mystical realm when you walk through it. Please note that, while there is nothing physically stopping you, cars are no longer allowed to drive along the road without special access. Stop at the designated carpark, then get out and explore on foot.

Next on the agenda, just 25 minutes down the road, is the even better-known Giant's Causeway – it's probably the most famous attraction in Northern Ireland, and inspired the name of this whole 130-mile (209-km) route. Composed of over 40,000 hexagonal basalt columns, formed 60 million years ago by cooling lava, the Giant's Causeway looks like a huge set of steps leading you out into the ocean. If you're inclined to believe local legend, it was formed by an Irish giant in a bid to win a war against his Scottish counterpart. Whether it's the battleground of colossi or a fascinating geological phenomenon, this bizarre natural wonder is most certainly worth seeing.

There is a well-signposted visitor centre and carpark by the causeway. It does get very busy, so if you'd like it to yourself we recommend going early in the morning, when you can watch the waves lap at the rocks in peace. Unless you're happy with an extremely early start, you might need to choose between this and the Dark Hedges if you want to avoid crowds!

Another 20 minutes down the road is Whiterocks, one of our favourite Causeway Coast beaches. Named for its white limestone cliffs and rock formations, its easy-to-find carpark makes it an accessible stop. If you are planning on swimming, try to come in the summer months when there's a lifeguard; you'll still need to be careful though, as the tides can be strong. It's also a great spot for surfing, bodyboarding and sea-kayaking (see page 207).

Half an hour further along the coast is Benone Strand in Limavady. A huge, golden-sand beach stretching for seven miles along the coastline, it's one of only a handful in the UK which you can drive on at low tide, making it the perfect spot to park up for a picnic lunch out of the boot of your car. This is a great option if you're on a budget; you can pick up supplies from a supermarket in Coleraine, yet still dine with five-star ocean views, spanning as far as Scotland on a good day. There are also a couple of local cafés that do nice coffee, cakes and lunch bites. In our opinion, Benone is the most spectacular stop on the Causeway Coastal Route, with its beach sandwiched between the long rolling waves of the ocean on one side, and the Umbra dune grasslands and clifftops on the other.

There are dozens of other amazing places to see along the route, each with its own unique blend of beauty, history and local hospitality. We suggest you take the 'slow road' along the Antrim coast when heading back to Belfast. As you traverse this Area of Outstanding Natural Beauty, you'll pass wild, rugged vistas, coastal towns and ancient forts and monuments. This alone makes it worth the journey over from the UK mainland if you're based there; combined with the rest of the charms of a leisurely drive along the Causeway Coastal Route, it makes one of the best road trips in the whole country.

Don't forget

If you plan on travelling via Belfast, we would highly recommend building in some time to stay a night here. We did so on the way back, and it was the perfect way to round off the trip. The city is particularly well known for its buzzing music scene; we'd suggest seeking out some traditional Irish folk music in a local pub, but if this isn't your thing, you're bound to find something. There's live music happening almost every night of the week, from glitzy gigs to laid-back open mic nights.

This circular hike through an Area of Outstanding Natural Beauty takes you through forests on your way to a mountaintop lake with views over the spectacular beaches of the Northern Irish coast and Magilligan Peninsula. This is one of the highest points on the north coast, making it one of the best places to get a sense of the majesty of this corner of the UK.

Time	few hours
Fitness	medium
Cost	free
Effort	medium
Equipment	none
Transport	car required

County Derry/Londonderry, Northern Ireland

Hiking the Binevenagh loop trail

Is this for me?

This loop covers three and a half miles (six km), and at no point is it too steep, making it a fairly easy route to tackle. You start along a tree-lined road before making your way through a coniferous forest, then up a short steeper section to the top. Personally, we love loop trails – you know you'll end up where you need to be, but without walking back through all the scenery you've already seen. The Binevenagh loop knocks it out of the park in terms of variety, with the way down feeling like a different world compared to the way up!

The route's highest point is a large plateau that drops off sharply at the cliff edge. For those scared of heights – be warned. If you can stomach the vertigo, though, this trip is well worth it for the views at the top alone. Still, it is possible to stay a healthy distance from the edge throughout, so you really needn't worry about falling off! In our opinion, if you're coming to Northern Ireland, you absolutely must add this to your itinerary.

The adventure

As with so many of these adventures, we really enjoyed tackling it at the crack of dawn. Sure, going early meant fewer people on the trail, but what made it feel really special was the sun rising with us as we hiked up the hill. What a start to the day – well worth one missed lie-in!

To join the route you must first drive to Leighery Road, inland of the northern tip of the Causeway Coast, where you can park your car. Keep an eye out for an obvious siding next to the sharp bend. From here, head southwest on foot along the Binevenagh Forest track. After 30 minutes, take a right to reach the 385-metre summit of the hill. It's an obvious turn-off point, so don't worry about missing it. Once you've reached the top, you'll be greeted by the sight of the lake which sits on the flat top of the hill.

If you're after that 'wow' factor, follow the lake shore around, and you'll see views right over the cliff's edge. The main landmark to look out for is the impeccable Benone Strand, seven miles (11 km) of uninterrupted sand, grassy dunes and dramatic cliffs along the coastline. The plateau where you stand is six miles (9.6 km) long itself, and was formed by molten lava over 60 million years ago. As you walk along the igneous rock, marvel at just how sheer the cliff face is.

Stop up here for your hot drink of choice and some well-travelled snacks. The panorama in front of you will beat any other spot, believe us. Word of caution, though – the wind is your worst enemy here. What was a lovely hike could become a risk to your life if a gust takes you over the edge. Be careful to keep your belongings weighed down while you're near the edge, and if the wind picks up, stay well clear of the cliff face.

After you've taken in your fair share of the view, turn tail to the eastern edge. From here, you'll find another well-trodden pathway, which takes you through another forest before arriving back at Leighery Road. This scenic walk is an excellent end to an exhilarating hike on the wonderful Binevenagh loop.

A seafood supper on the dunes at Runkerry

Perhaps one of the most exposed beaches on the Northern Ireland coast, Runkerry epitomizes the wild and rugged charm of the region, with its dunes offering a welcome reprieve from the elements. An evening spent cooking a seafood feast here while the sun sets over the ocean is one of the most peaceful slow adventures the UK offers.

Time few hours

Fitness low

Cost affordable

Effort medium

Equipment some recommended

Transport best by car

Is this for me?

This adventure requires some preparation in terms of sourcing the food and cooking equipment, which you will then have to lug out onto the dunes. You will also most likely have to make peace with the odd bit of sand making its way into your food, but this is a small price to pay for dining out in nature with show-stopping sunset scenes. For ease, a car would be useful, but buses do stop a short walk from the beach in Portballintrae.

The adventure

A sweeping sandy beach, tempting waves, undulating dunes and a Victorian-era manor house sitting proudly at one end of the bay make even a short visit to this beach memorable. But, if you have time, we found that cooking up a fresh seafood feast on the dunes really added something special to the experience. If you'd like to try it, you'll first need to get your hands on some ingredients. The closest fishmonger is Lir's, just under 20 minutes' drive away in Coleraine; just ask the staff for their recommendations, and you'll come out with deliciously fresh fish which works well pan-fried.

Once you have the makings of your feast, head to the little coastal town of Portballintrae; there's a carpark at its far eastern end. From here the walk to the Runkerry dunes is a short and obvious one as you follow the coast round, then take the little footbridge across the River Bush.

Runkerry is a 400-metre beach that almost always has waves, although surfing is not really advised unless you are experienced, as the rip tide can be dangerous. The grassy sand dunes offer the perfect place to set up your temporary kitchen. Take your time strolling along, before settling on a spot that balances views with shelter from the wind.

Now it's time to set up camp, kick back and cook up! If you are lucky and judge it right, you will be treated to a sunset show over the ocean as you scoff fresh fish and sip cold beers.

Tip: If possible, bring your own camping stove, frying pan and utensils, plus a rug to sit on. It's a good idea to put the fish on ice in a cooler, if you have one, just to keep it fresh on the journey. Coleraine has plenty of supermarkets and a greengrocer, so you can easily pick up anything else you might need on the day.

Don't forget

It's really important to leave no trace, so take care when packing up, especially as you'll be taking lots of bits and bobs which you could overlook. You might assume it's alright to leave some of your food waste on the dunes, but that's not the case. Take some rubbish bags, collect up all of your waste and dispose of it in the bin back at the carpark or take it home. That way we can keep our beautiful coastline clean, and preserve its magic for years to come.

Adventure Resources

This is your quick and easy reference for all the adventures – the items we have cursed ourselves for forgetting, the ones that we always end up leaving in our bags, the websites we use to check things like tides and weather, the rules and guidelines you need to know about. In other words, things we would have ended up writing 52 times if we covered them in each individual adventure.

Packing list

Forgetting a couple of items can really impact a trip, and it's completely avoidable with a bit of planning.

Each adventure is different, and therefore will require slight variations on what to pack. That said, we've compiled a list of core basics that we think should be in your bag for almost any UK adventure, whatever the season:

- Sturdy walking boots
- Small multi-purpose knife (with bottle opener)
- Lightweight waterproof
- Reusable water bottle – we recommend Ocean Bottle
- Picnic rug
- Swimwear
- Lightweight towel
- More socks than days
- Sliders/sandals for evenings
- Portable phone charger
- Basic first aid kit
- Matches/lighter
- Camping mugs

There are also a few non-essential items we're always glad to have with us:

- Portable outdoor light
- Portable stove
- A pot, plate and cutlery (per person)
- Camera

These are the basics, but as mentioned, naturally each adventure will require slightly different kit. In this book, if an adventure needs equipment beyond what we've listed above, we've made a note if it.

Apps

- **Campsites:** PitchUp and Nearly Wild Camping
- **Coastal water quality:** Surfers Against Sewage
- **Offline maps:** Maps.me
- **River water quality:** Safe Seas and Rivers Service
- **Tide times:** My Tide Times
- **Trails:** AllTrails
- **Unique accommodation:** Kip Hideaways
- **Weather:** Met Office

Responsible tourism

We know it's tempting to skip over this section – it doesn't sound the most exciting! But we think that it's not only important, but something which actually enhances your experience of the adventures in this book.

The term 'Responsible Tourism' is so overused by now that it's often viewed as just another box-ticking exercise for marketing companies. But when it comes to UK adventures, it's an essential part of both enjoying the landscapes and ensuring you don't diminish the enjoyment of other travellers – now or in future generations.

Dr Harold Goodwin, Director of the Responsible Tourism Partnership, puts it neatly and cuts through all the fluff: 'Responsible tourism is making better places for people to live in and better places for people to visit.'

These are the key principles we always try to stick to:

Leave no trace

This isn't a saying just for wild camping. It applies everywhere you go. Pick up all of your rubbish, including food waste, and take it with you. It's the least you can do.

Interact with local people

This might sound like a token gesture, but it's not. Having conversations with local residents will help you learn about the area's history and culture, make you aware of any important local guidelines, and sometimes even earn you tips on the secret spots most visitors don't know about... Try to consider yourself a temporary but active member of the community you're visiting, rather than an onlooker, and treat it with the respect you would your own home.

Spend locally

This is a good, simple and usually fun way to give a little back to the place you're enjoying. Rather than shopping at big chains, try to spend at small businesses. This empowers the local economy, and often means shorter supply chains with less transportation and packaging.

Go out of season

At peak season, a lot of places experience an unsustainable influx of tourists that cause traffic, overcrowding and damage to natural ecosystems. By visiting out of season you are not only easing this destructive issue but – we would argue – are more likely to have a better time yourself. You'll be able to explore beautiful landscapes without the crowds, which completely changes the experience.

Important rules and guidelines

In order to explore responsibly, there are a few pre-existing guidelines and codes you should bear in mind on your adventures across the UK.

Bothy Code

A set of guidelines published by the Mountain Bothy Association designed to ensure the bothies are looked after and left in good shape for the visitors after you.

Countryside Code

A set of guidelines published by Gov.uk that are designed for use by the public and landowners in England and Wales to help them responsibly enjoy parks, waterways, coast and countryside.

Open Water Swimming Guidelines

Useful safety tips from the National Water Safety Forum about wild swimming.

Scottish Outdoor Access Code

This provides detailed guidance on the exercise of the ancient tradition of universal access to land in Scotland, very relevant for wild camping today.

We just wanted to say a big thank you to everyone from our Travel Project community who has followed and supported our journey throughout the years. Clichéd cheese aside, without your tips, local knowledge, kind messages and support this book would never have been made. Simple as that. So, thank you very much – we hope you find the book valuable.

Also, thank you to the badass all-female team from Quadrille, for your patience and guidance throughout.

Quadrille, Penguin Random House UK, One Embassy Gardens, 8 Viaduct Gardens, London SW11 7BW

Quadrille Publishing Limited is part of the Penguin Random House group of companies whose addresses can be found at global. penguinrandomhouse.com

Published by Quadrille in 2024

www.penguin.co.uk

A CIP catalogue record for this book is available from the British Library

ISBN 978 1 83783 142 5

10 9 8 7 6 5 4 3

Managing Director Sarah Lavelle
Commissioning Editor Stacey Cleworth
Senior Designer Emily Lapworth
Photographers Charlie Wild and Jessica Last
Head of Production Stephen Lang
Senior Production Controller Gary Hayes

Colour reproduction by F1

Printed in China by RR Donnelley Asia Printing Solutions Limited

The authorised representative in the EEA is Penguin Random House Ireland, Morrison Chambers, 32 Nassau Street, Dublin D02 YH68.

Penguin Random House is committed to a sustainable future for our business, our readers and our planet. This book is made from Forest Stewardship Council® certified paper.

MIX
Paper | Supporting responsible forestry
FSC® C018179